Somebody's Angel Child
THE STORY OF BESSIE SMITH

WOMEN OF AMERICA

Milton Meltzer, Editor

TONGUE OF FLAME
The Life of Lydia Maria Child
BY MILTON MELTZER

LABOR'S DEFIANT LADY
The Story of Mother Jones
BY IRVING WERSTEIN

QUEEN OF POPULISTS
The Story of Mary Elizabeth Lease
BY RICHARD STILLER

PROBING THE UNKNOWN
The Story of Dr. Florence Sabin
BY MARY KAY PHELAN

MARGARET SANGER
Pioneer of Birth Control
BY LAWRENCE LADER AND MILTON MELTZER

SOMEBODY'S ANGEL CHILD
The Story of Bessie Smith
BY CARMAN MOORE

THE SENATOR FROM MAINE
Margaret Chase Smith
BY ALICE FLEMING

NEIGHBOR TO THE WORLD
The Story of Lillian Wald
BY IRVIN BLOCK

Somebody's Angel Child

THE STORY OF BESSIE SMITH

By Carman Moore
Illustrated with Photographs

Thomas Y. Crowell Company
New York

Acknowledgment is made to the copyright holders for permission to reprint portions of the lyrics of musical compositions listed below:

PAGES 23-24: "Walking Blues," by Ma Rainey, Northern Music Co., A division of MCA, Inc., 445 Park Avenue, New York, N.Y. 10022. All rights reserved.

PAGE 44: "See See Rider," by Ma Rainey, copyright © 1943 by MCA Music, A division of MCA, Inc., 445 Park Avenue New York, N.Y. 10022. All rights reserved.

PAGES 51, 70 and 107: "Young Woman's Blues," by Bessie Smith, © 1927, 1955 Empress Music Inc.

PAGE 69: "Down Hearted Blues," by Alberta Hunt and Lovie Austin, copyright © 1922 by MCA Music, A division of MCA, Inc. Copyright renewed 1949 and assigned to MCA Music, A division of MCA, Inc., New York, N.Y. All rights reserved.

PAGE 77: "Cake-walking Babies from Home," by Chris Smith, Henry Troy, and Clarence Williams, copyright © 1924 by MCA Music, A division of MCA, Inc. Copyright renewed 1950 and assigned to MCA Music, A division of MCA, Inc. New York, N.Y. All rights reserved.

PAGES 87-88 and 101: "Back Water Blues," by Bessie Smith, © 1927, 1955 Empress Music Inc.

PAGE 89: "Poor Man's Blues," by Bessie Smith, © 1930, 1958 Empress Music Inc.

PAGE 90: "Preachin' the Blues," by Bessie Smith, © 1927, 1955 Empress Music Inc.

PAGES 99-100: "Shipwreck Blues," by Bessie Smith, © 1931, 1959 Empress Music Inc.

PAGE 100: "Long Old Road," by Bessie Smith, © 1931, 1959 Empress Music Inc.

PAGES 103 and 107: "Nobody Knows You When You're Down and Out," by Jimmy Cox, copyright © 1922, 1929 by MCA Music, A division of MCA, Inc. Copyright renewed 1950, 1956 and assigned to MCA Music, A division of MCA, Inc., New York, N.Y. All rights reserved.

PAGE 106: "Please Help Me Get Him Off My Mind," by Bessie Smith, © 1928, 1956 Empress Music Inc.; and "Wasted Life Blues," by Bessie Smith, © 1929, 1957 Empress Music Inc.

PAGE 107: "Baby Doll," by Bessie Smith, © 1927, 1955 Empress Music Inc.

PAGE 108: "Death Valley Moan," by Bessie Smith, © 1929, 1957 Empress Music Inc.; and "Reckless Blues," by Bessie Smith, © 1925, 1953 Empress Music Inc.

DESIGNED BY ELKE SCHWARZ
Manufactured in the United States of America
L.C. Card 77-94797

1   2   3   4   5   6   7   8   9   10

To Martin Douglass Moore,
infant son and angel child.
Bessie Smith sang him
his first lullabies.

INTRODUCTION

My mama says I'm reckless,
My daddy says I'm wild;
I said my mama says I'm reckless,
My daddy says I'm wild.
I ain't good lookin',
But I'm somebody's angel child.

Many years have passed since Elisabeth "Bessie" Smith sang her blues for millions of cheering, enchanted listeners. The blues were new then, awaiting someone with the deep soul and musical genius to sing their curving melodies and longing cries the way they had to be sung. Those who heard her, with her head back slightly and her eyes closed, filling a music hall or traveling tent with sweet, full tones, will never forget it. Few members of those audiences remain. But the blues remain. The blues style is sung all over the world. That is why this story must be told—the story of the great lady who came to be called the Empress of the Blues.

ACKNOWLEDGMENTS

I would like to express my deep gratitude to the seventy-nine-year-old Jack Gee, through whose kindness I was permitted to enter the spiritual world of Bessie Smith for a time. He put at my disposal his excellent memory for dates, songs, and sentiments, most memorably in the fall of 1968 on a spectacular walking tour of old Bessie Smith haunts on Philadelphia's South Side.

I would also like to express appreciation to John Hammond of Columbia Records for his patient help in finding those few remaining people who knew Bessie and for his own bright recollections and encouragement.

Also valuable in my research were discussions with the great Louis Armstrong. Talks with the fine jazz scholar Frank Driggs were also helpful. Mr. Milton Kramer of Empress Publishing Company was of great assistance in my search for Bessie Smith manuscripts.

Martin Shulman and Brooks Kerr were kind and patient in their loans of out-of-print recordings. Mr. Shulman is also to be thanked for his photographs of Horan's and 1319 Christian Street. Meryl Joseph's early research aid was much appreciated.

In addition I would like to thank my wife, Susan, for having suffered many a lonely night and short dinner while *Angel Child* was being born.

CONTENTS

Somebody's Angel Child
THE STORY OF BESSIE SMITH

I
Scenes of
Bessie Smith
Growing Up Fast

Grinning Eagles

Bessie Smith came into this world with the blues. As a matter of fact, if you were born black in Chattanooga in the 1890's—and that almost by definition meant that you were born miserably poor—you had to be born with the blues. Elisabeth "Bessie" Smith was born into this world on the fifteenth day of April 1898 in Chattanooga, Tennessee.

Her mother's name was Laura, and her father's name was Moses. People said her daddy had been a preacher—dead before Bessie was out of diapers—that's about all they said about him. Mama Laura worked herself to an untimely death trying to feed all of the seven Smith children. Bessie was only nine years old when her mother died, and she and her favorite brother, Clarence, along with Bud, Tinnie, and Lulu, had to go live with her oldest sister, Viola.

It was all so terrible the day Mama died. Bessie

3

succeeded in blotting it out of her memory. But she remembered one thing to her dying day: the feeling that something didn't seem fair; something didn't seem right. That something was what they call the blues.

The year before Mama's death was an important one for Bessie. It was the year in which Bessie first performed on a stage.

She was little more than eight years old and almost good-looking in spite of the clean but frayed little dress she wore. She sat on the curb with her feet in the drainage ditch that ran along the street in front of the Star Theatre. The hot, late-afternoon sun beat down across her full, brown face, but she couldn't bother about that. Customers were already going into the Star for the weekly amateur show, and Clarey was late. He was supposed to have gone after his guitar and gotten back so they could run through the song they were scheduled to sing. How she wanted to win that prize! One dollar! And that dollar could be put away toward the purchase of some new, ball-bearing roller skates.

The word, the very thought of, roller skates carried Bessie away on daydream wheels. She saw herself flashing through the streets of Chattanooga, the neighborhood kids shouting and trying in vain to run alongside her. She saw herself pass the fashionable downtown stores where white folks who had come to

4

shop would have to jump out of her way. She could almost hear them exclaim in whispered voices, "That must be little Miss Bessie Smith, the queen of all singers . . . the one who won the dollar on the Star Amateur Show."

"Bessie, what're you doin' sittin' there dreamin'?" shouted an excited and real voice in the real world.

"Doggone you, Clarence. You're gonna make us lose that prize," Bessie shot back with a snap of her head. "Let's get on in there."

And off they ran . . . tried first to run through the audience entrance . . . were rudely herded out by the ticket taker and sent around to the side door marked "Artists' Entrance" . . . rushed into the darkened backstage area and came to a sudden halt at finding that a dancer was already on stage dancing his heart out and that eleven more acts were waiting.

It was a long afternoon and a long evening. Jugglers, jug band players, singers singly and in groups, comedians—all at least twenty years old—talked over what they were going to do, fidgeted, or just lounged in the corners. Acts came and acts went. She couldn't take her eyes off all that she was seeing. Performers who had looked mean and dissatisfied in the wings would suddenly burst into smiles when the curtain went up and belt out some happy song, only to scowl and curse at the audience or the piano accompanist under their breath after the curtain was down again.

After the many long weeks and even years she and Clarey had sung and danced on street corners for pennies, after the many tent shows and show bars they had sneaked into to watch, how mystifying it seemed to be seeing the real world of performers as they prepared, performed, and came off exhausted, exhilarated, or ashamed. As the evening wore on, her ears began to register less and less the sounds of piano, Swanee whistlers, and singers and more and more the sounds that crowds make—hisses, angry yelling, and only occasionally but with a sound like a mighty river the sweet roar of applause. The crowd, the great animal that wants to be moved . . . . The moment that frightened her most happened after an old comedian had gone out there and done his act and was met by nothing but silence.

But something had happened backstage there to the by-now overwhelmed Bessie Smith. She began to see in show business what a gambler sees in the race track. It had something to do with taking chances. And the feeling began to creep over her that this is what she wanted and that she had finally found her home. She began to forget that dollar. She wanted a crack at that audience. And she wanted to come away with the real prize . . . applause.

"Clarence, he's going to say our name! Wake up, Clarence!" squealed Bessie, shaking her dozing brother.

"And now, ladies and gentlemen, our final contestants—Clarence, who will pick the guitar, and little Miss Bessie Smith, who has something she wants to sing for you . . . ."

Bessie let out a little screech at the sound of her name and the audience's welcoming applause. It was like the cry of some young hunting cat that had sighted its first prey. She rushed on dancing.

Nobody's Child

"Come on, everybody. See what four feet can do. If you ain't big on dancin', well, we'll pick and sing for you . . . ." Heard on a street corner outside a little barbecue shack next to a roller skate rental—Chattanooga, Tennessee, 1907.

Yes, it was Bessie—back on the streets again. The other two feet referred to were those of Clarence, who shuffled about as he beat away at his guitar, while Bessie tapped and brushed on her rented roller skates. Imagine! The Star Theatre's amateur champions of the week applauded and shouted over last week; this week, back on the street corners; last week, a dollar for one little song and a tiny bit of dancing; this week, a whole day's song and dance for a total of about ten cents. With ten cents you could rent roller skates for about a day. The roller skates were due back. Bessie turned them in, paid the man at the counter, and headed slowly home with Clarence.

They were hungry. There might be food at home, and there might not be. Mama Laura had been sick these last months and went to work only when she could. When Mama didn't work, she didn't get paid. And when she didn't get paid, dinner times were sad affairs, at best consisting of biscuits sopped in *Alaga* syrup. At worst, there would be ashcake corn bread and dandelion greens seasoned with a piece of salt pork—maybe. "Maybe" means if there was any salt pork left, and "maybe" means if the right kind of dandelions were growing; because seven kids, no matter how hungry they might be, can't pick what isn't growing.

"Look, Bessie," yelled Clarey. "Let's grab us them potatoes." Purfoy, the vegetable man, was closing his shop across the street, and the contents of his outdoor bins had almost all been carted inside. Five potatoes sat there with "The Smith Children" all but written on them. Purfoy was nowhere in sight. Bessie and Clarence broke suddenly and headed over on a dead run. Bessie grabbed two and Clarence had two and was reaching for the last when Purfoy came flying from his store swinging a bushel basket and cursing loudly.

"Git yo' black hands offa them potatoes," and with one smack he knocked Bessie over the curb into the muddy street, her potatoes gone forever. With a hard clout of his basket Purfoy then fetched Clarence a blow on the back that made him drop his potatoes and almost dislodged the precious guitar from the

9

strap around his neck. The youngsters took to their heels, ran a block or two, then slowed to a dejected walk.

"You got yours?" asked Bessie after a block of silence.

"No. You got yours?" responded Clarence.

"Rolled into the street," said Bessie.

Clarence fussed at making a knot in his broken guitar strap. I've got a sad evening on my hands, now, thought Bessie. Usually she was so busy getting together pennies on the street, or daydreaming about adoring audiences and owning nice things like ball-bearing roller skates that would belong to her alone, or using her wits to avoid getting a licking from Mama, that she didn't have a lot of time to think of how desperate she really felt most of the time. But every once in a while a mood would descend on her that made her almost feel like giving up. Usually she was a fighter. She would talk up to her older sisters when she felt they were hounding her. She would even punch any neighborhood boy in the nose, if he tried to take advantage of her. But when she got those moods—those blues moods—when that gray cloud seemed to fall around her mind, she would just sit and think of all her trials one at a time, and as trial piled up on tribulation, she would reach a point where she just wanted to be a baby again and turn herself over to somebody's unquestioning love and care.

Bessie always liked to be clean and look neat, but now her dress was muddy and ripped on the side.

10

Mama Laura, being tired and ill, was very hard to live with these days—very irritable and quick to give out with the lickings. And to tell the truth, Bessie didn't feel very good about stealing from Mr. Purfoy. She was hungry, that's all. "I've got the blues, and I can't be satisfied." Those words that she had heard sung by a lady called Ma Rainey drifted through her mind.

Bessie sighed deeply as they arrived at the street of dilapidated shacks where they lived. Clarence looked around and started to ask her what was wrong, but deciding that he knew the answer to that, he went on. As they approached the house, Bessie's big sister Tinnie ran out of the front door toward them. "Clarey, Bessie, there's a white man here to see you!"

"Clarey, the police!" yelled Bessie, ready to run.

"What's wrong with you, girl?" said Tinnie. "That ain't no police. He says he heard you at the Star Amateur show and wonders if you'd sing at his theater . . . for money . . . eight dollars." Bessie and Clarence yelled and ran inside.

Bessie Smith made her professional debut at the Ivory Theatre in Chattanooga. She earned her eight dollars that week and did what her nine-year-old heart told her. She bought a brand new pair of ball-bearing roller skates. But she paid double for that purchase. When she arrived home that night, Mama Laura waited at the door for the week's wage that she hoped would see the family through the next week or

11

so. When Mama Laura saw the shiny skates in Bessie's hands, she asked, "What's that?" Bessie told her. Mama took out her switch and gave Bessie her full wrath and drove Bessie, her face streaming tears, out of the house. Bessie was so angry and frightened that, once outside, she just kept going and wandered for hours, not knowing where to go or what to do. Not daring to return and too full of young pride and fury to return, she found herself far from home. As a matter of fact, she was now at the edge of town down by the Tennessee River and not far from Lookout Mountain.

In Chattanooga you could up and see Lookout Mountain from any spot in town. Now it seemed that Lookout Mountain was looking down at Bessie. It seemed neither to smile nor to frown. Like a bad audience, it only sat there as if waiting for something more important than Bessie's problem to occur. If it was talking, it was saying, "Who cares?"

As usual, Bessie was hungry, but there was nothing she could do about that now. What bothered her was that she was becoming so terribly sleepy, and she was so cold her back was shimmying. Somebody's farming shack was not far away. Bessie crept up to the building. It was dark, and if anyone was living there, they were asleep. She slipped around to the back, looking for anywhere she could shelter herself and sleep. An outhouse was what she found. A cold wind that had been blowing down the river valley brought rain. Bessie went into the cramped shelter and fell asleep on its broken, wooden floor, but before she slept, she wept again. It was still raining in the morning when she trudged home. She found it hard to forgive her mother for that night.

Not many weeks after that, Mama Laura sat down in the living room chair and died. The Smith children moved into the house of their sister Viola, who already had a child of her own almost Bessie's age to raise and not much money to do it on. Bessie had always been pretty much on her own, but Mama Laura had at least always looked after her. Now no one in her family seemed to pay much attention to her, except when they thought she needed a licking. To all of her brothers and sisters, except Clarey, Bessie was trouble. She wandered around town alone late at night and got into fights with the neighborhood children. The Smith children had one other brother named Andrew, who was grown up and worked at the local jail as a turnkey. Many was the night that he saw Bessie wandering around and chased her off the streets.

She felt she had no home. Her parents were dead. She was nobody's child.

A Lesson
in the Blues

Bessie had the blues. And we're talking about the real blues here, which means that she didn't just feel a little downhearted. That she had the real blues means that she was lost in her sadness. It means that she was sad *again,* sadder than she ever dreamed she could be. It means that the sadness that had really always been lurking around her door was knocking again, and that, somehow, she'd just have to outlast it. And after this bout with the blues passed, she would have to get down on her knees and pray that it would never come again—pray that a change in her life was coming, though all the time suspecting that that heavy blues feeling would never really be gone forever. Well, although trouble was never going to leave Bessie Smith alone, that change in her life was not far off. Bessie's shield against the blues, strangely enough, was going to be a thing *called* the blues, and

14

a plump, friendly tent-show singer by the name of Gertrude Malissa Nix Rainey was going to show her the way.

Blues, of course, is a mood—that mood of hopelessness that Bessie, with her mother gone, her brothers and sisters mistreating her, and her stomach empty much of the time, was suffering through. But the word blues, also, after the Civil War and the setting free of black slaves, came to be the name given to a new form of music that those freed slaves were creating. At the time of their freedom, which jubilant black folk called the Day of Jubilo, these new freedmen expected a new day—a change in their lives. They thought, though they had no jobs and wore little more on their backs than the rags of slavery, that they could now think of white folks in America as their brothers and sisters. They thought that now whites would be just brothers and sisters in Christ and country who would help their black brothers until they could get the learning, homes, and employment it would take to get on their feet in this pioneering land. But much as Bessie's own brothers and sisters had behaved toward her, whites seemed to turn their backs and only look in the black man's direction when they needed someone to do backbreaking labor or someone to treat badly.

Black freedmen felt deserted and hopeless and had many occasions to feel *blue*. The feeling was so common among the people that they used to refer to the

blues as Mr. Blues. As they had sung religious spiri-
tuals and field-work songs to lighten their load as
slaves, now as freedmen, often jobless with hungry
families, they expressed themselves even more plain-
tively and directly with the new blues songs.

At first, since most black folks had been slaves in
the rural South, the blues was the "country" blues,
sung by blind men and wandering farm laborers who
accompanied themselves, mainly on the guitar. But
by 1900 many blacks were finding menial labor in
cities like Chattanooga, Atlanta, Chicago, Philadelphia, and New York, and the children of the old
people who once had entertained them in rags at barn
dances were coming to the cities with more elaborate
shows, new forms of entertainment, scenery, and
flashy costumes. F. C. Woolcott's Rabbit Foot Minstrel Show was one of the oldest and most popular of
these traveling shows.

Show business was one way a black person could
make fairly good money, and traveling shows were
always looking for good entertainers, especially
singers. Gertrude Nix had been discovered at fifteen
years old by the manager of one of the Rabbit Foot's
several troupes. His name was Will Rainey, and he
decided to marry the young singer and take her with
him into the hard but exciting life of show business.
Ma Rainey, as she came to be called, knew, as few
other big-time performers seemed to know, that what
her audiences after a hard day's work would most

16

need to hear would be the blues. With the piano players and instrumentalists that accompanied the Rabbit Foot Show, she began to work out a new, more big-time way to project the lowly blues to her homesick fans in the towns and cities. Her audiences loved it. She sang about bad luck and trouble. She sang about poor men who left their families. She sang about love affairs that didn't work out. She sang about her audiences' lives. Hearing her, many black people, especially young people, wanted to learn to sing blues the way Ma Rainey did, but whereas almost everybody likes to sing and can sing a little, not everybody is *born* to sing.

Bessie Smith could sing. It was clear to all who heard her, whether she was performing on a street corner or at the Ivory, Bessie Smith was born to music. Chattanooga, in that year of 1909, was a bustling, bursting new railroad town, and Bessie and Clarence were not the only people in the streets hustling for the coins of the many workers anxious to be entertained and diverted there. But Bessie stood head and shoulders above most of the other street urchins, organ grinders, and patent medicine performers who frequented the streets of Chattanooga. Young Bessie's powers of musical communication allowed her to turn busy shoppers into hushed and often adoring audiences. And on the stage her strong but sweet young tones turned audiences, just out for a light evening's entertainment, into roaring congregations.

17

Ma Rainey heard Bessie one night and didn't forget it.

"I want that little street gal in my show," said Ma to her husband, Will, in a very determined voice. "Look here, Will, I ain't no kidnapper, but you know as well as I do that if she's left to run the streets day and night, somebody's not takin' very good care of her. I don't need to tell you that." She looked out of the corner of her eye for some go-ahead sign from Will. "Yes, I saw her perform down at the theater, but I've also seen her four times since . . . . I saw her lurking around outside this very wagon twice. I saw her and her brother once over on the corner of Gilmer Street singing and dancing. And once I ran into her way on the other side of town in the dead of night." Will Rainey grunted and that was all. "She's got a very nice little voice," mused Ma. "Spunky little old girl. Of course we'll have to leave her brother here. I'm going to teach her to sing with our musicians. What if we use her after that opening dance chorus number?" She had clearly made up her mind as she turned and said, "We don't have no tent to put up here in Chattanooga, so I'm going to call a couple of those roughnecks and send them out after that child. All right, Will?"

Will Rainey, all the time seated at his rickety desk, had hardly paid much attention to what Ma had been saying. He was the boss of this troupe of the Rabbit Foot Minstrels and had many duties of a business nature to perform every day. The show had finished its stand in Chattanooga, and today was payday. "You do what you want to do, Ma," said Will, hardly turning.

"Hey! A couple of you tent men come here," boomed out Ma from the door of the rented show trailer. "Joe and Son, let them cards be for a while. I've got a little job for you." Joe and Son couldn't have pretended they didn't hear her even had they been playing blackjack on the top of Lookout Mountain. Ma Rainey had the most powerful lungs in show business.

Bessie at eleven years old was large for her age, and she knew how to throw a right-hand knockout punch like a man. Kidnapping her was like trying to tie up a wild stallion with a strand of spaghetti. Anyway, Son and Joe, after a whole afternoon's search and a sunset hour's worth of cuts and bruises, dumped a burlap bag full of cursing, outraged Bessie Smith on the floor of Ma's dressing wagon.

"Thank you, boys, I really appreciate this," said Ma with a half smile.

"Don't give us that mouth full of much obliged, Ma. We want a day's extra pay," yelled Son.

"Yeh, and we'll be on our way soon as we get it. This show life's got just too rough for me, anyway," Joe joined in.

Ma didn't care. She paid them and didn't even see

them leave. What she was watching with a strange fascination was a tiger of an eleven-year-old girl fight her way out of a bag. First came feet, then a rear end, and finally a defiant and furious face topped by totally disheveled hair. Ma readied herself for a big fight, but Bessie, seeing her, stopped in her tracks and just glowered. Many folks on her block would have been surprised to learn that Bessie hadn't torn into Ma with her fists flying. Bessie just didn't feel like fighting this lady.

Bessie's face began to relax and take on a look that was less evil than surprised. So this was the famous Ma Rainey close up! Bessie had heard her sing once and liked what she'd heard. Bessie was also feeling a bit too tired to really fight. But maybe the main reason for her restraint was a notion that this squat, motherly-looking woman was going to look after her.

"I hope those roughnecks didn't hurt you. I want you in my traveling show. Get yourself a couple of blankets from that trunk and lie down over there in that corner," said Ma in a firm but not unfriendly voice. Bessie just stood there looking meeker by the moment. Just then the wagon gave a sudden lurch and Bessie found herself on the floor.

"No turning around now, Bessie Smith," Ma said, trying not to show how relieved she felt. "Them horses are pulling us to Georgia. We'll do our talking in the morning. I'm going to teach you the blues, gal," and with that Ma turned off the coal-oil lamp that swang from a peg above the rickety desk and disappeared behind the curtain that separated the office space from the Raineys' sleeping area.

Bessie crawled around and found the trunk and three rough-woven blankets by the light from the street that spilled rhythmically through the tiny wagon window as they moved. She threw two blankets into the corner. She fell exhausted upon one and covered herself with the other. She lay looking over at the window for a while. Just then it began to rain softly, and a flurry of thoughts came upon young Bessie as she started to realize what had just happened. Ma Rainey, the greatest blues singer in the world, had just had her stolen from her home town. Clarence was being left behind. She missed him already. Vi, Lulu, Bud, Andrew, and Laura, her family . . . . They were pretty mean to her—took the money she earned and gave her beatings for any little thing. They were left behind, and, well, she missed them, too. So why didn't she really feel sad?

The light was no longer coming through the window. Chattanooga, the birthplace of her blues, was falling behind the line of wagons that hauled the famous old Rabbit Foot Minstrel company over the Tennessee State line. Going to Georgia . . . . Bessie hadn't traveled much outside Chattanooga. She remembered having spent a short stretch of time in Memphis, where she sang with a little church choir. What an ugly-looking old woman Ma Rainey was to be so famous, thought Bessie, as the motion of the old wagon rocked her gently and the rain popped against the trailer top. She felt her eyelids go heavy and her cheeks and lips slide away into sleepiness, and the words of Ma Rainey returned as a dream, "I'm going to teach you the blues. I want you in my traveling show. I want you in . . . . I want you . . . ."

Day after day as Bessie rehearsed her number Ma would sit by the piano and correct, scold, and demonstrate. "There is a right way to sing the blues," she would say.

THE BLUES

A.   Sing one line.
B.   Now sing those same words, and start on a new note.
C.   Sing new words, and start on a new note.
      That was called the first chorus.
      Do it all again with totally new words.
      This is called the second chorus.

SINGING THE BLUES RIGHT

1.   Let the instruments or the piano do what they're going to do, just as long as that beat is firm.
2.   Slide that note.
3.   Let that last note be full and strong, but let it also cry.
4.   Let that piano work all through your melody: talk with him.
5.   Be a horn, but be the main horn.

A LESSON IN THE BLUES

FOR A SAMPLE

FIRST CHORUS— Woke up this mornin'. Woke up
this mornin',
With my head bowed down.
Hey-Hey-Hey.
Woke up this mornin', With my
head bowed down.
I had that mean old feelin'
I was in the wrong man's town.

SECOND CHORUS— The mailman's been here. The
mailman's been here,
But didn't leave no news. Hey-
Hey-Hey.
The mailman's been here, But
didn't leave no news.
That's the reason why
Mama's got the walking blues.

FIRST CHORUS Woke   up   this   mor - nin'.
SECOND CHORUS The   mail - man's   been here.

Woke   up   this   mor - nin'___   With   my
The   mail-man's been here,   But didn't

23

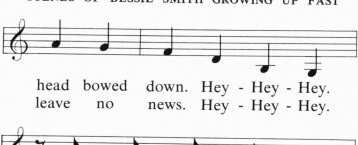

head bowed down. Hey - Hey - Hey.
leave no news. Hey - Hey - Hey.

Woke up this mor - nin'___
The mail - man's been here___

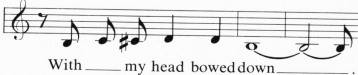

With ___ my head bowed down ___.
But did - n't leave no news ___.

I had that mean old feel - in'___
That's the rea - son why___

I was in the wrong man's town ___.
Mama's got the walk - ing blues ___.

24

That is a representation of what Ma Rainey began to show Bessie as Will Rainey's Rabbit Foot Minstrel troupe wound its way eastward through Georgia from town to town, at times moving by wagons and, as years passed, by railroad. But most of Bessie's blues education resulted from listening backstage as Ma, dressed to the teeth in show jewelry, feathers, sequined gowns, and resplendent wigs, would bring the house down night after night with a big voice rich as wine. Bessie came to realize that the kind of blues Ma sang was audience music. Ma's crowds listened and made approving sounds while she sang, just as if the songs belonged to them, as if the blues song could never be a completed thing without the audience. Ma's performance was like being in church with Ma the head preacher.

Ma Rainey's Show Gal Daughter

Bessie was starting to feel good. It is true, however, that those first days after the kidnapping were not easy for her—inside, that is. Bessie always, ever since she could remember, seemed to be having little wars going on inside her: she loved Mama Laura but she also hated her; she loved her block back in Chattanooga but she hated it; she felt she'd better be tough, but she felt that the real Bessie Smith was soft as mud deep in her heart.

On that morning after having been carried off, Bessie recovered some of her sass and had a whole mouthful of cuss words ready for Ma Rainey when she got up. And the rumpled little urchin delivered that mouthful with all the venom she could muster. Bessie cussed, kicked, and cried. Ma just stayed busy and a step out of the way until the hot-eyed youngster cooled a bit. Ma figured that Bessie was just behaving dead-center like star material and without that fire wouldn't last very long in this walk of show business. Crying, kicking, and misbehaving were a good part of what the blues were about, she figured, so she let Bessie rail.

Along toward noon, as the wagons ground to a halt at the edge of a little Georgia town, Ma came from behind the curtain and announced to Bessie, "We're going to pay you for your services here, so don't carry on like you're doing us a favor. If I took a mind to it, I could slap the fool out of you and send you back to your gutters in Chattanooga. You keep hollering about your family this, your family that: I saw you running the streets hungry in the dead of night. Was your family looking after you? Huh! If they notice you're gone a month from now, I'll be surprised. We're going to pay you two dollars and fifty cents a week, and if you want to give me your family's address I'll send a dollar of it to them. Anyway I bet they used to take your little street change from you and then give you a lickin' for not bringing more!"

Bessie was astonished into wide-eyed silence, just as she'd been the night before. It was true what Ma had said—Vi and the others had taken her money from her and given her lickings. Still, Bessie loved them and feared that they might go hungry without her help. "Ma," she said, all the time liking the notion of saying a mother's name again, "could you send a dollar fifty home and pay me a dollar?"

Ma Rainey stopped a moment, a bit taken aback. She studied the eleven-year-old face, which had softened to that of the child she really was. Ma had not expected to find any softness or generosity in this big, tough girl. She's going to be a great star, someday, thought Ma.

"Come here, gal, and give Ma some sugar," Ma said, opening her big, fat arms to receive the little girl. "Of course, honey. If that's what you want, that's what Ma's gonna do," and she bear hugged Bessie, who was already taller than she. "Now go on out and get yourself some breakfast. Ma's got to dress up for the parade through town. You're not going to be lonely. You're part of Ma's family now, and I think you're going to like it here. Wipe your eyes now and fix your hair before you go out. That's it. And get yourself a little dress out of that trunk over there." Yes, Bessie was feeling fine.

The parade through the little town's Negro section made Bessie's blood race until she thought she would choke. She had seen traveling shows come through Chattanooga and she'd always been filled with excitement by them. The little bands blowing their heads off, horses and wagons rolling by, country blues men with guitars, jug players and comics, long-legged dancing girls covered with ostrich feathers, and the stars of the shows glowing with smiles in their self-assuredness—all would pass through like a mighty river in the sun. The last show parade she'd seen was these same Rabbit Foot Minstrels, run by Will "Pa" Rainey and starring the great Madam Ma Rainey, back in Chattanooga. Now, Bessie herself was a marcher and saw the cheering spectators as she was going to be seeing them for over twenty years— from the performers' procession.

At the center of the black quarter the parade paused and the tumult stopped. Pa Rainey climbed atop the main trailer and made a big announcement about where, when, and what the show tonight would be. He introduced his jugglers, who flipped a few bottles between them as the mystified townsfolk oohed and ahhed. He called attention to his dancing girls as the men in the crowd whistled and made all kinds of sounds. And as Pa Rainey talked up the Rabbit Foot show, the performers did splits, mugged, and generally whipped up the crowd. Then Pa Rainey called attention to Ma and the crowd went wild. Ma Rainey was loved all over the South, and people waved and called to her as if she were a relative returned home. Then the procession continued to even faster and sassier band music than before.

Bessie hadn't been pointed out individually, but she did bow with the youngsters of the troupe, so she felt at least half appreciated and very important. Children and their dogs pursued the column and Bessie found herself growing a bit sad, remembering that just a few weeks ago she and Clarey had run at the tail end of the Rabbit Foot parade and had several times sneaked up to the parked trailer of Ma Rainey for a peek at the great lady. The thought passed swiftly, and before she knew it they were pulling into a field, and the roughnecks, of which there

were many, had pulled a huge canvas out of one of
the wagons and were preparing to set up the show
tent.

The main tent went up so fast it looked to Bessie as
though it would flap once or twice and fly away. And
all around and in and out of this monster made of
cloth roughnecks, performers, musicians, feathers,
straw and horses rushed, laughed, and yelled like a
new world was being created.

For Bessie that's what it was,, a new world. She
stood alone, staring, with a smile flickering about her
full lips. She stood alone at the roadside edge of what
a moment before was a quiet field, watched only by
birds and distant trees. Now she stood alone near a
crowd of hilarious, mad people in a space that might
as well have been the moon, watching her new world
rise. Bessie was starting to feel good.

"Bessie! Come here, child." It was Ma, who came
flying out of the tent suddenly like a flesh cannonball.
"Go on in there and rehearse your song with the
piano player. We got a show this evening." Bessie
liked that and soon became just another part of the
pell-mell scene unfolding in that Georgia meadow.
The birds and pine trees saw her break into a run.
They watched her run into the big canvas pyramid to
become part of Ma and Pa Rainey's strange and wild
family. They watched her go into a tent to prepare an
old song, like "Stack O. Lee" or "Frankie and
Johnny." They saw her, but they did not understand

30

that she was going into a new world—that a change had come to her life.

This new world was exciting, but it was not a child's world. Bessie had to learn fast and grow up fast—faster than she would have liked to grow up. The performing was not the hard part: she had been performing almost since she could walk. The problem was the people. She didn't always dislike all the people. A part of her loved the roaring crowds, the challenge each new audience represented, the sweetness of being loved and respected. And yet there was another Bessie Smith who just simply got tired of people. There were so many of them, so much pressure from them. You traveled with people. In a small town with no hotel, you had to stay overnight with a strange new family. You were in crowded dressing rooms with people. Some of those show people would steal your clothes and your money. You needed to work things out with the musicians so your songs and dances would work right. You had to please the audience. You had to take orders from the Raineys. Sometimes you had to fight people.

No, the Rabbit Foot was not heaven on earth. Bessie in her few years with the show often saw men —usually the roughnecks—slash one another in furious razor and knife battles. She saw show people, Ma herself at times, drink themselves silly and not be able to perform. And, speaking of Ma—Ma was always good to Bessie and was the closest thing to a second mother that Bessie had ever met. But one day Bessie found out that Ma hadn't been sending money home to Bessie's family at all. Bessie became furious and heartsick at that disclosure. An awful scene took place that night. Bessie recovered from the incident, but was always a little more suspicious of people than she would like to have been after that.

In its wide rovings the traveling show offered other annoyances that Bessie had to learn to overcome. One of them was due to the fact that she was becoming a good-looking teen-ager with a solid little body. Grown men frequently would grab at her, and she'd have to fight them off with her famous right hook. Some of the young girls in the troupe were not so able to fight—nor so willing.

This was not the first time she had lived in the middle of such turmoil. Chattanooga was a railroad town, and her old neighborhood had been full of tough men and drifters. But Bessie had thought that those had been the ways of the old world, the world she'd left behind. Little by little she was starting to think that after all there was only one world and that it was a hard one. The Rabbit Foot was just another country. Its main value was that Ma Rainey was its queen, and it was she who held the secret to the new blues.

II
The History of Bessie Smith as a Teen-Ager Making a Name for Herself

The "81" and the Cotton Pickers

Bessie hadn't spent much time in school. The Chattanooga Board of Education hadn't seen fit to arrange an elaborate education for black children, and for a little girl who was black, schooling was thought to be a waste of time. She learned to read and write a little, and that was about it. Yet, her learning never stopped. For almost three years she was a member of the Rainey Rabbit Foot Minstrels, and for learning the ways of show business there wasn't a better place. Three years with Ma was like six years of college for a student as quick and serious as Bessie Smith. By the time she was thirteen she had learned many a dance routine (she was never great at it but she could dance), she had learned hundreds of songs —everything from standard minstrel tunes to the blues—and she had learned valuable extra points, such as how to "sell" a song before an audience, what to do with your hands, and how to breathe so that your voice was strong enough to send the notes out into all parts of a huge tent or auditorium.

There was one more lesson that being in the Rabbit Foot organization taught and taught well—how to look out for yourself. How to get to the dinner wagon before other hungry show people got there first and ate up the food. How to make sure the publicity poster had your name on it in a prominent spot and in large enough letters. How to keep your dresses and money from being stolen. How to make a weekly salary of a dollar buy you the good things in life, such as candy and soft drinks. These lessons Bessie learned, with the exception of stretching the money. Bessie Smith was not in her whole life going to learn how to hang on to her money. Just as she had bought roller skates with her first big pay back in Chattanooga, she spent her money whimsically now as a thirteen-year-old. She liked a dress, she bought it. Fellow performers soon found that she'd lend them money without a single protest and that she seldom demanded to be repaid.

Of course Bessie was not the only young singer in the U.S.A. learning to sing Ma Rainey's brand of blues. Many a young girl heard Ma sing them as the Rabbit Foot show rolled across the Southland, and a growing number of blues singers were at work in black show business. But Bessie felt that she was going to be the best of them. She itched to improve, and she itched to show to the world what she could do. It was as if Bessie herself were the blues and it was as if they both had to move on to reach every black person in America. Bessie did break loose, but how it happened was a surprise, even to her.

The show rolled into the bustling city of Atlanta, Georgia, one day in 1911. Atlanta was fast overtaking New Orleans as the big-time show town of the South. Several theaters existed, and money, which was always scarce in black communities in those days, was fairly available there. Opportunity filled the air. In a large town the Rabbit Foot show would play a local theater rather than having to put up and perform in the tent. The show's entrance, as usual, was in parade but a parade of extra vigor with far more brightly colored costumes and shimmering feathers. By now Bessie was a featured singer, and unknown though she was in Atlanta, she was given special attention on the posters put up on Decatur Street where many of the show theaters were.

The Rabbit Foot's stay at the new "81" Theatre in Atlanta was long and successful. Bessie's singing and tall, young good looks did not go unnoticed by the audiences. One man in particular, Charles P. Bailey, who managed the "81" Theatre, did more than notice the talented teen-ager. On the last night of the Rabbit Foot's run in Atlanta—after all their bags had been packed and loaded on the train—Bessie Smith was kidnapped and hustled to the office of none other than Charles P. Bailey. The Rabbit Foot rolled out of town and Bessie's stint with them was ended forever.

Charles P. was a white man. He was also bull-headed and could be evil-tempered. He had a keen nose for business and a good ear and eye for talent. His "81" Theatre was, along with the smaller and less elegant "91" Theatre a few doors up Decatur Street, a virtual magnet for the crowds of Atlanta black folk out for an evening's excitement. In addition to his show business position, Charles P. Bailey was a tax collector and connected with the sheriff's office and city politics.

That confrontation between Bessie Smith and Charles P. in the "81" office can only be imagined, but since Bessie was second to none in the hot temper department it must have been quite a showdown.

Whatever happened, Bessie agreed to stay and perform for Bailey, but there was a catch. In spite of the success the "81" experienced when big-name shows such as Will Rainey's played a stretch there, business over the whole year was not very good. Charles P. was still paying off old debts and informed Bessie that it was going to be hard to get a show together for her to perform in. He had wanted to organize a troupe of young girls no older than Bessie to sing and work up some dance routines centered around her. Bessie, though not more than thirteen, knew a lot about show business by now, thanks to Ma. She liked Mr. Bailey's idea and wanted to make it work at all costs.

"What if you advertise for some girls to act in the show and buy some cloth and feathers for costumes?"

said Bessie like an old-timer. And Charles P. did just that. So Bessie moved into an old rickety shack that stood out in the backyard of the "81" Theatre, fixed it up neatly, and, once the young girls began arriving, began to lead them in designing and sewing up costumes. She pleaded and scolded and drove the would-be children's chorus tirelessly. After they left for home—since they were all from Atlanta—Bessie continued to sew in her little one-room shack. When rehearsals began, Bessie was a leader. And by the close of the opening-night show it was clear that the "81" had a hit, one that would run for a long time. Little girls dancing in short skirts, mocking their elders, plus the already popular and talented Bessie, brought the customers rushing into the "81." Charles P. Bailey was obviously pleased, but like Ma Rainey and many others Bessie would soon encounter in show business, he didn't show his good feelings by paying Bessie more than a paltry few dollars a week.

Charles P.'s teen-aged son Tom, a lanky, jug-headed but friendly sort, was at the theater constantly accompanying his blustery father. He liked and was awed by Bessie from the beginning, and the two of them became fast friends. So it was on many an evening at dinner time that under the big old tree in back of the theater, Bessie and Tom would make a fire and roast corn and hot dogs on a stick. Often the other girls from the show would join them, and then it would be like a birthday party out there. Looking over her entire childhood, you could say that Bessie

Smith was raised to adulthood in back of theaters, in tents, and on the streets—a strange, new breed of outdoor girl.

Bessie remained at Charles P.'s "81" for almost a year. At fourteen years of age she began to look so much more like a young woman than a child star that it became clear that the act would have to be disbanded. Charles P. Bailey was powerful and becoming successful, but the real kingpin of the black entertainment circuit down South was Milton Starr, who headed the T.O.B.A. T.O.B.A. stood for Theatre Owners' Booking Association. It was Milton Starr who actually scheduled and negotiated which singer and which show would play in which town or theater. When he became aware of the talents of the blossoming young Bessie Smith, he hired her, and she found herself on the road again—this time with a group called Pete Werley's Florida Cotton Pickers. She also found herself earning the same peanuts. In spite of her growing name and popularity, she was paid only $2.50 a week by Mr. Werley. Well, Bessie loved her singing and performing more than she loved money, so she decided not to complain. All the performers felt a bit shortchanged by the T.O.B.A. system. Some jokingly said that T.O.B.A. stood for "Tough On Black Artists."

Anyway, off they went, often by train, at times in trucks and show trailers, through Alabama, Florida, Mississippi. Bessie just did what she had to—sing her songs with all she had in her, learn everything that passed her way about show business, and send her audiences home whistling and excited about what they'd seen and heard her do.

The blue mood—Mr. Blues, that wretched feeling—was not hounding her too much these days. She was young and attractive, and she was starting to learn about young men and falling in love. With the Cotton Pickers she usually sang to the accompaniment of one piano. The pianist at that time was a brilliant young man by the name of Clarence Williams. Some say that a romance developed between the two, but no one knows for sure. At any rate, although she soon left the Florida Cotton Pickers and traveled on her own, the artistic collaboration between Clarence and Bessie was just beginning. And whether she was a changed young lady or not, her renditions of all those blues songs that spoke of men and women and a love affair were deeper and fuller and sung with an urgent meaning she had never given them before.

Young Woman's Blues

Bessie Smith was a young woman now. She could cook a bit; she chose and bought her own clothes; she could catch a train and go where she had to go for her next show; she could fight off any insistent man she did not like; and she could lure almost any man she did like. She was only nineteen years old, but she was as grown up and experienced as someone twice her age.

In those days—that was 1917—black teen-agers had to learn quickly how to take care of themselves, how to earn their living, and how to prove their worth. There was little hope of being sent to college to prepare for careers as teachers, doctors, or social workers. Blacks were not often taught typing or business skills.

A situation called segregation existed across the entire South, which the white people there enforced in many ways. A black person could not go to the white public school, ride in the same railroad car with whites, eat in the same restaurant, or sit next to a white person in the movies or vaudeville theater. When shows such as the Rabbit Foot Minstrels or the Florida Cotton Pickers played a town, they would have to play a midnight show once a week for whites only called the "Midnight Ramble." If a black person broke too many of the segregation rules, he might be put in jail or lynched by a mob of whites, which meant that the mob would take the black person into the fields or woods and kill him.

Black folks were allowed and encouraged to work at certain jobs. Building buildings, taking care of children, preaching in churches, collecting garbage, sweeping and mopping in white homes, cutting timber, and farming were important jobs for black people. And there developed a furious competition to get them. Black folks called this competition "scufflin'." But the plum situation—the job that was most respected and held the most promise of wealth—was show business. Hundreds, maybe thousands of young people who could sing, dance, juggle, tell jokes, or play an instrument—even a little bit—would dream about becoming a performer and would try to break in with a show. Everybody black was not a natural; Bessie Smith was. But show life at times was as hard as farming.

One of the hardest aspects of being a young person in show business was the question of falling in love. It was almost impossible for Bessie to think of getting

43

married and settling down, when to make a living in show business meant you had to keep traveling. Bessie fell in love probably many times, as young girls do, but she always knew it wouldn't last. Men were like wild, flying creatures who came to earth to feed and then were gone. Bessie too became like a creature in flight—looking for the nest, calling out in song, but always leaving the nest behind.

After leaving the Cotton Pickers, Bessie had roamed the South alone. Often in touch with Milton Starr, she worked the T.O.B.A. circuit some of the time. But finally she found herself going from cabarets to hole-in-the-wall saloons to local dance halls. She sang such songs as Ma Rainey's famous "See See Rider." This was the small time, and this was a lonely time, but she sang her heart out each night.

See See Rider, see what you done done.
You made me love you, now your gal's done come.
You made me love you, now your gal's done come.

I'm gonna buy me a pistol just as long as I am tall.
Gonna kill my man and catch the Cannon Ball,
If he don't have me, he won't have no gal at all.

It was a rough time for her, but even during that time when she found herself working in little drinking spots on the Gulf of Mexico or maybe in a miserable old Alabama town, she would feel, strangely, at

44

home, as if these noisy, hard-drinking dock workers and their women were part of her family.

On a Friday night, after the workers had drawn their week's pay, those little joints would smell of fried fish and beer, and people would be staggering about and falling over chairs and yelling to their friends. On a Friday night there was bound to be a fight between two women or two men over some mutual lover and everybody would duck under the tables as a gun went off or great, big shiny knives would swish about bent on blood. On a Friday night there would also be laughter and poking of fun at some guy, wild dancing, and somebody dressed in slick clothes with spats on his feet and a cane in his hand saying, "I love you forever, Baby."

Bessie became part of this life. She didn't know any other nor did she seem to care, as long as she could sing the blues and as long as her listeners loved her. She danced in those night spots, she fought and danced with those people who were out trying to have some kind of fun after a week of backbreaking labor, she laughed with them under the low, smoky lights. But she learned one thing from them that was going to make her life miserable—she learned to drink gin and Scotch whisky and to love it.

One night she wandered into a small interior Alabama town called Selma. She had been told by somebody on the way to Selma that she might get a singing job at Min Murphy's. Bessie asked around town for

45

its whereabouts and found herself before a large but beat-up sort of building. When she went in, she was met by a full-bodied but tired-looking blond, who wore, it seemed, nothing but a thin robe over her body.

"I'm Min Murphy," she said, exhaling a breeze of whisky as she announced it.

Bessie had taken a job in Selma's red-light district. As the afternoon passed, men in sharp suits or overalls came and went, and women giggled from the house's interior. Bessie dressed for her performance that evening. She had decided to work that night and get out fast. But she was a proud singer, and once on the little barroom stage platform, she prepared as usual to sing her best.

There are several ways to sing the blues. You can talk the blues, you can shout the blues, you can sing them naturally, and you can moan the blues. That night Bessie stood up front near her piano man and moaned. As she sang, certain words just disappeared into pure humming sound. Sliding slowly, the long notes reaching out for one another in her fine dark soul, she became at such times a singer no more, but a burnishing saxophone or a trombone of the gods.

A white man had slipped into the ramshackle bar and seated himself in the back as she sang the blues. He remained there transfixed into the night. He had to get to see this creature and talk to her. But when Min went after Bessie, who'd left the stage some time before, she found that Bessie had gone. The man

46

left quietly—disappointed, but with the name and staggering young talent of Bessie on his mind He felt somehow that he would see her again and that if he could, he wanted to let the world know that talent. He was a music promoter and recording man from up North. His name was Frank Walker.

Several years passed, and Bessie wandered. Her reputation in the South was growing and she was making more money. Bessie liked the fact that so many people were getting to know her name. She felt less lonely now going into a new town to perform, because she knew that there'd be at least a few people there who'd heard of her and were glad she was coming. Of course there were also people who knew that she was a blues singer but were *not* glad she was coming to town. These were usually the upstanding, church-going folk. Many church people in black communities had only scorn for the blues. "The blues is the music of the Devil, and those who sing it are surely going to roast in Hell," the little preachers would shout from their pulpits. Being the daughter of a preacher, although she never really knew her father, Bessie always felt a little bit uneasy about this feeling some folks had about her and the blues she loved. She didn't go to church herself, yet she still didn't like being thought of as a "bad" girl. But she'd shake off her unhappiness about this with a toss of her head . . . . "Huh, they're there praying on Sunday, and on Monday they're back at their sins." And on

47

she would go, singing the songs that pleased her—the songs that were about life as she knew it really was.

Life as it really was was the First World War now raging over in Europe. Life as it really was was millions of black people, poor and fighting to have a little fun at least once a week. Life was trying to find somebody to love who would love you. Life was her family at home in Chattanooga that she longed to see once more.

She returned to her Chattanooga family once when she was just turning nineteen years old. Bessie had always tried to send as much money home as she was able to. Now she wanted to see her brother Clarence, especially, and Vi, Lulu, and Tinnie and Bud and her nephews and nieces. The only one she had seen in the last eight years was Bud. Bud had become desperate for money and gotten mixed up in robberies and other crimes. In trouble with the law, he had found Bessie one day while she was performing in New Orleans with the Rabbit Foot show, and she'd given him what she had. It was Bud who'd disclosed to her that Ma and Pa Rainey hadn't been sending her salary home.

Bessie arrived to a warm reception. Everyone in the family was buzzing about her success and wanted to hear stories of her travels. It made Bessie feel good to no longer be considered the bad girl of the family. Tinnie had given birth to three boys in the years since Bessie's leaving. And Vi's daughter Laura, who was almost Bessie's age, had had a son. But her beloved

Clarence had already left home and was trying to make a career for himself in traveling shows. Right at this time he was in Kentucky working on the tents— a roughneck for a medicine show. He had given up his guitar for the time being and hoped for a chance to become a comedian and maybe do a little comic dancing.

Bessie was glad to hear that Clarence was in show business, but she was also sad at not seeing him. And that was not the only news that was to make her sad. Bud was dead. Bud, next to Andrew, was her oldest brother. Bud had been shot in Louisville, Kentucky, by the police. "How did it happen, Tinnie?"

"Well, you know . . . he was always in trouble with the police. It was only a matter of time before they'd have gotten him, anyway."

Bessie felt a little dizzy during the few days at home. Home. This was not her home, and she knew it. Her home was the road and the tents and the nearest hotel to the theater she was working in at the time. Bessie wanted to get out of Chattanooga and she wanted to get Vi and Tinnie and their families out of there before they went crazy, or before one of her nephews grew up and perhaps began to steal for his existence and maybe got himself shot down with a stolen purse or a potato in his hand.

The money she had at the time wouldn't get the family to the other side of Lookout Mountain. Bessie caught the next train out of town. She had decided to return with new vigor to show business. She had decided to make her name and make money—and make that money talk. She was now absolutely determined to become the queen of song. Her present destination was Atlanta—on her way to the stars. But as she flashed along in the car marked "Colored Section," and watched the poor farms, the mules, and the shacks fly by like rivers and clouds, she had to claw and fight with Mr. Blues—hoping that he wasn't going her way.

"Steppin' On Out"

No time to marry, no time to settle down.
I'm a young woman, and ain't done runnin' roun'.

Some people call me a hobo, some call me a bum
Nobody knows my name, nobody knows what I've
   done.

I'm as good as any woman in your town.
I ain't no high yaller, I'm a beginner brown.

I ain't gonna marry, ain't gon' settle down,
I'm gon' drink good moonshine and run these
   browns down.

See that long, lonesome road? Lawd, you know it's
   gotta end.
I'm a good woman, and I can get plenty men.

Bessie got to Atlanta, and Bessie got tougher. She was
determined to enjoy her life. She laughed louder, and

she drank harder. She saw to it that her name was put up on those signs just so. And she saw to it that show people with whom she was not close friends called her "Miss Bessie." She carried herself a new way—like she was the best. And she wanted to be paid like the best. She began to buy bright new dresses and jewelry.

One day Bessie got in touch with Milton Starr and told him that she was going to form a show of her own. Since the First World War had just ended in a victory for America and its allies and since her show would tour the South, where a young lady was called a "belle," Bessie decided to call her production the Liberty Belles. It would be a razzle-dazzle, happy show with lots of gay costumes, bold and large-framed dancing girls, and plenty of laughs for the customer. The Liberty Belles went on the road with the T.O.B.A.'s blessings, and the show was an instant sensation. From Atlanta and Asheville, North Carolina, to New Orleans the show spread the name and reputation of Bessie Smith far and wide. People not only wept and swayed to moaning blues such as the hit "St. Louis Blues," which Bessie poured forth with such fine new assurance, but they fell out laughing at the comics, the big chorus girls, and Bessie singing such hokum songs as "Those Dogs of Mine," a song she had learned from Ma Rainey.

Look-a here people, listen to me,
Believe me I'm telling the truth.

52

If your corns hurt you just like mine,
You'd say the same words too.

Out for a walk, I stopped to talk,
Oh, how my corns did burn,
I had to keep on the shaded side of the street,
To keep out the light of the sun.

In those days if the audience liked a performer, they would throw money onto the stage. That almost always happened when Bessie sang, but some people say that when she was a little low on cash she would station helpers out in the audience to start the money throwing. Immediately the audience would be dipping into their pockets and filling the air and the stage with coins and wadded-up bills. Bessie would walk regally off to her dressing room as if she hadn't noticed. Of course, since she was becoming a queen, she would never pick up a cent of it herself. Instead she'd send a musician or dancer out with a bag to collect it, saying, "Sugar, go pick up that money for me, and take some for yourself."

Bessie was out touring the South with the Liberty Belles, and alone upon occasion, for much of the year 1919. Southern black audiences were lovers of a good time. When they liked a performance they were loud and enthusiastic in their approval. Under their burden of hard work and oppression they were usually kind to one another, but to their star performers they were almost worshipful. All the rest of her life

53

Bessie would call these Southerners "my people."
Going South she always called "going down home."

The year 1919 passed. The "roaring twenties"
were beginning. The war had been over for more than
a year. The United States was getting richer by the
minute. People of all races seemed to have more
money and better jobs than they had had before
World War I. They wore brighter and snappier cloth-
ing, and when they dressed up they wanted somewhere to go and something to do. Up North, centered
in New York City, new theaters were opening and
presenting plays and musical comedies written by
such composers as George M. Cohan, Irving Berlin,
and Jerome Kern to larger audiences than ever before. Movies had been invented by Thomas Edison,
and, although they were still silent movies, accompanied by lone piano players, crowds lined up to get
inside. Everybody was dancing, and the old cake-
walk and turkey trot were moving aside for the
shimmy, the Charleston, and the black-bottom. Jazz,
which had been around for thirty years or more, was
wedding ragtime and the blues into a style of music
that would make peoples' feet refuse to stop dancing.
This was 1920, and many things that would
change the life of Bessie Smith were occurring. Although she would only use it once for her own
work, public radio would be first appearing that year.
Into Harlem in New York City would stream thou-

sands of black soldiers who had been born in the South, and who were returning from Europe—soldiers who would become an audience homesick for the good old Southern blues. Another of Edison's great inventions, the phonograph machine, was going to be important to Bessie. And although it had been around for over twenty years, it would just this year record its first blues singer—Mamie Smith (no relation to Bessie)—singing "Crazy Blues," and sell a million copies. Also of direct interest to Bessie in 1920 was the bad news that Congress was enacting a law against the sale of liquor. People called it Prohibition. It meant that if Bessie and millions of others like her wanted their gin, they would have to get it illegally from men called moonshiners who made their own booze when the police weren't looking, or they would have to sit around drinking in secret bars and nightclubs called speakeasies.

Though the majority of black Americans since slavery had lived in the South, by 1920 it was clear that the action—the jobs, a fresh chance at success, and the fun—was moving north. Bessie got a call from a show place in Atlantic City, New Jersey, and she packed her bags immediately and caught the next train, determined to conquer the sophisticated North.

Atlantic City soon knew about her. A busy vacation spot on the ocean, Atlantic City was the home of many an entertainment spot. Bessie stayed there singing, drinking, and enjoying herself for two years.

Dance halls with names like The Board House, Paradise, The New World, and Kelly's kept her busy. And she became friends with singers, dancers, and comics with names like Coffee, Madison Reed, Bert Wheeler, and Half-Pint Jaxon.

The town was jumping, and Bessie was one reason for it, yet she longed for some traveling and more money. In spite of her artistry and crowd appeal, she was making only fifteen dollars a week in Atlantic City. She was not long in finding a traveling companion. Back into her life one night came the pianist and song writer Clarence Williams, and Clarence had big plans. For one thing, he had already written a hit song called "I Wish I Could Shimmy Like My Sister Kate." Bessie learned it quickly and was ready to put it to work on tour. For another, he had made some connections with the Columbia Recording Company and had arranged for Bessie to go to New York for a tryout. Bessie had tried out earlier that year with the Emerson Company but had been turned down, and she hated for anyone to turn her down. Yet the thought of trying again to get a record company interested in her made sense to her.

Blues singers were springing up all over the country. Mamie Smith, Sara Martin, Alberta Hunter, and others were becoming big blues names through the recordings they were making. If Bessie was going to really be the queen and really show what her talent was, really strike it rich, she knew she must make records. She decided to hold off on the tryout: she was a little too upset by her previous failure, and she wanted to move into some new territory. Philadelphia was the town she chose, and though she didn't know it then, her life was about to turn a cartwheel. Bessie Smith was going to find her lover man.

III
How Bessie
Came to Be
Empress

Jackie Gee

"Who's that big policeman over there at the bar?" Bessie asked Dimples, her backstage helper at Horan's Cabaret on Philadelphia's South Side.

"That's Jackie Gee, Miss Bessie. He won't bother ya none. He just drops in from time to time to watch the show and keep the cuttin' and shootin' down to a minimum," said Dimples, giggling.

Bessie was peeking from behind the narrow curtains that hung at the door between the dressing rooms and the room where the customers ate and danced. In spite of Prohibition Bessie could see clearly that many in her audience were either drinking their liquor or had already finished. Bottles of all descriptions lined the tables. Horan's, at 13th and South Streets, was known in Philadelphia as a wild place, second in reputation only to the Madhouse. Bessie was a little nervous, not so much because of the unruly behavior of the customers in the darkened room: she worked her share of wild places. She was uneasy because she, a countrified Southern girl, was making her first appearance in a really big northern city. Since Atlantic City she had already sung in a few small towns in Ohio and Pennsylvania, and the audiences hadn't been as enthusiastic as she had wanted. If small towns had been a bit cool to her, what could she expect of the third largest city in the U.S.A.? People up North didn't seem to like to sit and listen as much as they liked to do the new dances—the Charleston and the shimmy. Anyway, it was time to go on.

Bessie and Dimples walked out onto the tiny platform at the back of the cabaret, but nobody even looked up. The noise continued unabated. Bessie stood there in a plain street dress, firm of body and regal in spite of the simple dress. Dimples informed the piano man that Bessie was onstage and ready to begin, then sat down. The piano broke into "There'll Be a Hot Time in Old Town Tonight," and Bessie looked out into the room and saw her would-be audience still laughing and shouting—everyone, that is, except the tall policeman at the bar, who smiled as his eye caught hers across the room. Bessie went to Dimples' table, took her glass of whisky, and drank it down. Then she went back onto the little platform of a stage and stopped the pianist. "I want it quiet in here!" she yelled out in a voice made powerful from a lifetime of singing.

The room fell silent with men the size of oxen turning suddenly toward the platform with astonished faces. "Start your song there, piano man," she said royally. And what a show she put on. Her voice soared out through the room for song after song and when it was over, the crowd didn't want to let her leave. Bessie turned and went through the little door toward the dressing room with money raining down on the stage behind her.

In the dressing room she was visited by a short white man with a limp. It was Charlie Eazel, who managed Horan's. He was all out of breath. "Bessie, Bessie . . . ." he panted.

"Miss Bessie," she corrected.

"Miss Bessie, you were fantastic. I want you to stay for a month. As a matter of fact you can stay a year," he said.

"I don't know, Mr. Eazel. This town is a little fast for my blood, and anyway, I like to keep moving."

"Well, can you stay at least another day? There's a fine young guy out there, a policeman named Jack Gee. He asked me to ask you if you'd have dinner with him tonight after he goes off duty."

Bessie sat a moment looking into her mirror. "Tell him yes. I'll meet him here at the cabaret," she said, unable to stifle the little smile that played across her lips.

It was not that easy, though. Suppertime came, and Bessie got the news from Eazel, more out of breath than previously, that Jack Gee had been shot while chasing a hoodlum by the name of Bad Sidney. He was in the hospital, seriously wounded. Bessie rushed off to see him. It was in the long series of thirty-four daily visits to Jack Gee while he lay in the hospital— at first near death and then little by little regaining his health—that she began to fall in love and realize that she had found her man at last.

The young policeman, too, was falling in love, and Bessie's mother-hen concern for him was clearly a big help in his recovery. In fact when the day for his release from the hospital came around, Bessie's care almost killed him. Jackie was taken home to his three-room apartment on the corner of Warnocke and Bainbridge, and Bessie went right down to the food market and bought pork chops, collard greens, cornmeal, black-eyed peas, and all the trimmings. Bessie was already an excellent cook and made a meal fit for a king. Jackie ate like a hungry wolf. The next day Bessie received the information that Jack Gee had burst his stitches and was back in the hospital. He had simply eaten too much.

He recovered quickly, though, and a short time after returning home again, Jackie was on his feet and very much in love with Bessie Smith. By this time Bessie had been asked by Clarence Williams to come to New York for a tryout with the Okeh recording company. Well, the truth is that Bessie Smith was broke. No matter how she came to be broke—she may have given her small wage away to the street urchins in the neighborhood; she may have spent it on moonshine liquor; she may have bought food and

Bessie Smith

*Ma Rainey and the Rabbit
Foot Minstrels*

Ma Rainey as she toured with the Rabbit's Foot Minstrels vaudeville show.
Her accompanists were Gabriel Washington, drums;
Al Wynn, trombone; Dave Nelson (King Oliver's nephew) trumpet;
Eddy Pollack, saxophone and Thomas A. Dorsey (Georgia Tom) at the piano.

Horan's Cabaret, 13 South Street, Philadelphia, where Bessie and Jack met

Jack Gee

1319 Christian Street, Philadelphia, where Bessie and Jack were married

Bessie and Jack as newly-weds

To-a-Pal

Bee Holland

Bessie
Smith

Studio

things for Jack with it—she couldn't afford the train fare to New York, and she didn't have a decent dress to wear. Jack looked at Bessie slyly. Then, without a word, he left the little second-floor apartment and went for a walk in the neighborhood. When he returned he had the money. He had pawned his watch and who knows what other valuables. And Charlie Carson, who owned a little record store and who was already a fan of Bessie's, had thrown in some of his savings to buy Bessie a black beaded dress in the latest fashion.

Bessie went up to New York City—the apple, the capital of the music kingdom—and she made her test record, "I Wish I Could Shimmy Like My Sister Kate," with Clarence Williams at the piano. How she did sing. Clarence called it in later years the greatest record Bessie ever cut. But after it was all over the Okeh producer thanked Bessie and sent her back to Philadelphia.

Bessie came home to Jack, disappointed but still certain that her real break was not far off. Her popularity and fame on Philadelphia's South Side grew and grew. She took the Madhouse by storm. Soon she was playing the Standard Theatre, the most important show place in the area.

In New York changes were also happening at Columbia Records, which ran the Okeh company. The old manager and producer at Okeh were being moved out, and none other than the Irishman Frank Walker, who had been so moved by Bessie's singing

65

many years before in Selma, Alabama, was taking over. And he hired Clarence Williams to be his assistant. Frank Walker's first order of business was to send Clarence on the next train to Philadelphia to get Bessie Smith up to New York. "Go down there and find her, and bring her back to me," he commanded.

It was early in 1923 and when Clarence arrived in Philadelphia, Bessie and Jack were already talking about a wedding. They decided to postpone it until spring. The next day Bessie and Clarence were back on the train to New York. This was it. This time she was not going to fail. Little Miss Bessie Smith was on her way: the prize was going to be the empire called the Blues.

Session to the Top

"Let's go through that again, Clarence. Bessie, you'll have to stand closer. Yeh, sing right into that horn. We're staying at this thing until we've got a perfect take. 'Down Hearted Blues' sung by Bessie Smith— it's going to knock this country right on its ear. Okay. Take number four," announced Frank Walker. The little recording studio of Okeh Records rang to the sounds of "Down Hearted Blues" for the fourth time that day.

Recording was in its early days. There were no microphones then. The singer stood before the large mouth of a big, black horn and sang into it. The vibration from the singing rattled the cutting tool, or stylus, at the small end of the horn and made the proper grooves in the "master" record. Copies of the master were made by machine in the record factories and shipped to stores all over the country for sale.

Records made especially for sale to the black pop-

ulation were put under the label of "Race Recordings" and were sold in barber shops, cabarets, cigar
stores, drugstores, and by mail, as well as from record
stores, for seventy-five cents. Phonograph machines
were heavy, wind-up affairs with a horn sticking out
to send out the sounds. The black people of the nation
went wild buying these machines, often spending
their savings or pooling their money with neighbors
to make the purchase. They had to hear the blues. An
ever-growing parade of blues performances followed
Mamie Smith's "Crazy Blues" onto phonograph records during the early twenties, but there still were
only a handful of real hits. If a guy asked for a long,
slow haircut and maybe a shave in 1923, he might
get a chance to hear all of the recorded blues hits in
existence by the time the barber was through with
him.

Bessie had managed to remain scared through all
four takes. As a matter of fact she had recorded
"Ain't Nobody's Business If I Do" that morning and
had felt shaky then, too. She felt that she had good
reason for her nervousness. After all, she had failed
her former tests, and she didn't want to let Frank
down, not to mention Jackie and all of her fans back
in Philadelphia and down South. Also she knew that
"Down Hearted" was written by the young blues
singer Alberta Hunter, and she knew that Alberta
had already recorded it and scored a hit with it.

"Hold it, Clarence. Bessie, you're still shaky.
You've got nothing at all to be afraid of, honey.

You're on your way to becoming the greatest blues singer anywhere. Take a moment and get set," said Frank in his kind but music-wise manner.

Bessie fidgeted there a moment in the little antiseptic studio, then lowered her head and sent her big notes rolling down into the horn:

"Trouble, trouble . . . I've had it all my days.
Trouble, trouble . . . I've had it all my days.
It seems like trouble gonna follow me to my grave.

I ain't never loved but three men in my life.
I ain't never loved but three men in my life.
My father, my brother [and] the man that wrecked
my life."

There was a story in those words—part of Bessie's own story—the story about the trouble, the man, and the grave. But Bessie at the time knew only that the session for that day was over, that she was very tired, and that she felt better now than when she'd entered the studio. The next day she returned to the studio, strong and unafraid, and cut "Gulf-Coast Blues," which Clarence had written for her to occupy the other side of the recording. Frank Walker was overcome. A star was being born. That country moan from Selma that had so moved him many years ago was going out to be shared by millions of people. Bessie returned to Philadelphia with $125 in her pocket, and the promise from Frank Walker of many more recording dates to come.

It was April 7, 1923, and Bessie was feeling weepy as she walked slowly beside Jack along tree-lined Christian Street in Philadelphia to the Reverend Tensley's house at number 1319. In spite of twenty-five years of hard times and worldly ways, she looked fresh and innocent like a little girl on her way to communion. It had been a long time since she was last in front of a preacher of any sort, but today the preacher was going to do something that must have seemed miraculous to her. The Reverend Tensley was about to join Bessie Smith and Jack Gee in marriage.

As she approached the door of the old flat-faced house she thought of a snatch of blues lyrics and giggled:

No time to marry, no time to settle down.
I'm a young woman, and ain't done runnin' 'roun'.
I'm a young woman, and ain't done runnin' 'roun'.

They were married that day and drove over to their new apartment at 1226 Webster Street for the reception. Friends, fans, and well-wishers dropped in to congratulate the couple all evening long. Laughter and liquor flowed freely and a good, hot down-home meal of fried chicken, collard greens, black-eyed peas and corn bread, pigs' feet, and candied yams was served to everybody. Bessie kept looking over at Jackie as if she didn't believe it all could be true. She wished that Clarey, Vi, Tinnie, and the rest of her family could be there. The feeling that something was amiss in the universe didn't bother her now. She sang and danced in a new way that day and that evening with her friends laughing and kissing the bride and with her new husband—tall and kind—pressing her hand from time to time. It was as if the universe were trying to pay her back in happiness for what it had brought her in tears.

Bessie also thought of the fantastic career that had just opened up for her. The sales of "Down Hearted" and "Gulf Coast" were on their way to the million mark. Theater owners and the T.O.B.A. people were crying for her to make a tour immediately.

The next day she and Jackie took off for a honeymoon in New York City. From the very beginning Bessie couldn't keep herself from buying gifts for Jack. Whether he protested or didn't, she would bring him whatever she could afford and whatever she thought he would like. A ring, a shiny new watch, a cane with a golden knob—she wanted to thank him for their love, she wanted to make him feel good. And Jackie loved his big, country girl in a way he had never loved, as the two of them gawked, strolled, and cut up in the great big city that was the capital of music.

Hardly had their honeymoon begun when Bessie received a call from Frank to come over to Columbia to record "Beale Street Mama" and "How Come You Do Me Like You Do." After an assured and exuberant performance on that "honeymoon session," Bessie collected her $125 from Clarence Williams.

He had arranged things so that Columbia paid him $250 out of which he paid Bessie what he wished.

Jackie stood there in the studio office for a moment and thought. "What does the contract say, Bessie? Are you contracted to Columbia or to Clarence?"

"I believe I'm supposed to be paid by Clarence," she answered.

Jack disappeared into Clarence's office. For a few minutes there was the sound of one man attempting to scramble under a desk in order to escape the wrath of another man who was yelling at the top of his voice. Jack reappeared, then went into Frank Walker's office. When he returned he informed Bessie that a new contract was on its way and that henceforth she was working directly for the Okeh division of Columbia Records.

Bessie had been signed by the T.O.B.A. for a triumphal tour of the South to last ten weeks. She was to make $350 a week and start in Atlanta at Bailey's "81" Theatre. Bessie hired a pianist and the famous dancer Carrie Nugent to fill out her show, and away she went leaving Jack on his beat in Philadelphia. She didn't like that—leaving Jack behind. But she did like the idea of returning in glory to old theaters where a few years before she'd performed for a dollar fifty a week.

When she arrived in Atlanta huge crowds were out to greet her show. And all week she performed five times a day to packed houses. As she proceeded from Pensacola, Florida, through Mobile, Alabama, to the

Frolic Theatre in Birmingham and back to Atlanta, where the impatient Jack Gee joined her, Bessie became increasingly amazed first at how many people had heard and been thrilled by "Down Hearted Blues," and secondly at the great magic of recordings as a means of reaching into the nation.

Once in Chattanooga, where the tour was to close, Bessie went immediately to the rickety two-story house where Vi and Lulu lived to present her new husband to them. Tinnie lived across the street and sold bootleg whisky for a living. When she heard Bessie was at Vi's, she dropped everything and came running over with her children. Neighbors hung out their windows for a glimpse of the great new singer, and Bessie's nieces and nephews were in her lap and hanging from her neck almost before she had a chance to sit down. After the show that night Sam Reaven, who was Milton Starr's partner in the T.O.B.A., came to Vi's house to discuss another ten-week tour with Bessie. "Same deal, Bessie, three hundred and fifty dollars. This time you'll move further west . . . ." said Sam.

"Different deal, Mr. Reaven," broke in Jackie. "Different deal. Bessie has had to pay one hundred dollars out of that measly three hundred and fifty to Carrie and her piano man, while your circuit here is cleaning up. We've got a contract to play in Detroit for eleven hundred dollars and we're going up there."

Jackie had learned something important about Bessie by now. She was a master of the blues, but she didn't know a thing about money. He had heard so many stories from her of how the Raineys hadn't sent money home as they'd promised, how on the Pete Werley Minstrels Show people had stolen money and clothes from her. Now, with her great popularity filling theater after theater, the circuit was willing to pay her rent or buy the dress she might want. Something in Bessie Smith didn't respect coins and dollar bills. That something inside her seemed to say that fine talent always would be rewarded by the heavens with whatever it needed. Well, if the heavens worked that way, Jackie thought, they had worked it this time by sending him to look after Bessie.

"Quit the police force, Jack, and come on tour with me. I'm going to miss you too much, Baby. Let's form our own show and tour with it. You'll be manager," Bessie pleaded.

Jack thought about it, but not for long. "Finish up in Detroit, and we'll try to arrange it," he answered. "It's worth a try. Maybe we can send for Clarey."

Bessie Was
the Queen
and Became
the Empress

Bessie was feeling good. Their new show, the Harlem Follies Troupe, was now a reality. Jackie, bitten by the show-business bug, had been all over the East gathering talent. Twelve dancing girls, a six-piece band, two comics, a ballet dancer, and the great one-legged dancer, Peg-Leg Bates, were going out on this show. Now they were in Harlem's Lafayette Theatre going through the final rehearsal. Bessie had demanded better and better performances during rehearsals—both of herself and the company. These last few months she had never stopped insisting on excellence.

What made Bessie especially happy about the line-up of talent was that one of the men they had hired as comedians was her brother Clarey. The two men she loved most in this world—Clarey and Jackie—were going to be with her on tour. She found it hard to control her joy, and as a result she began buying presents for both.

Bessie had many friends in Atlanta by now, and when the show got to that wild old town, there were mobs of well-wishers out on the street for the parade. Bob Hamilton, the piano man, sat and played in the hot fashion on the back of a gaily decorated truck while the band and the performers played and strutted on behind. "There'll Be a Hot Time in Old Town Tonight" thrilled the summer crowd on Decatur Street and drove the hundreds who had planned to be at the "81" anyway to rush to line up at the box office early. Before show time, Bessie and the whole Follies troupe had a neckbones and black-eyed peas dinner at an old friend's house.

The hostess's name was Lou, but show people called her Pot of Peas. Feeding that crew was quite a task, because show people had voracious appetites. The dancers, for instance, were in perpetual motion during a day of at least three performances. When they played small towns, Clarey not only had to act as Master of Ceremonies and head comic but was also in charge of getting twelve canvas men to assemble the tent. That meant a lot of stakes had to be pounded by even the boss of the roughnecks. Jackie and the musicians had less strenuous work to do during a show, but they just seemed to like to eat anyway. Bessie could be forgiven any amount of collard greens and corn bread she wanted to wolf down. She did everything in the show—danced, often did comic routines and said lines, and of course tore the place up singing her songs.

Not all of Bessie's songs in these shows were blues. And not all of her blues were sad by a long shot. She sang a straight musical-comedy number called "Old Broadway Melody." She also sang, "Get a working man when you get married / Let all these pinchbacks be." And to much laughter from the crowd, she would sing, "All my life I've been making it / All my life white folks have been taking it." At the end of the performance the entire company would strut and swing down to the edge of the stage as Bessie sang her own hot Charleston-style composition, which went:

Here they come, look at them demonstratin'
Going some, look at 'em syncopatin' . . . .
Cake-walking babies from Home.

And at that point the crowd would go wild.

Pot of Peas and the Atlanta audiences were not the only Southern home folks to roll out the red carpet for the Harlem Follies. All summer of 1924, as they went west and north across the country, enthralled crowds stood in lines to see the show. Though recording was important to Bessie, touring performance was what she really considered the true artistic challenge. She rehearsed, scolded, and polished the musicians who accompanied her until they played a rock-steady beat and musical lines that built up to hers.

For those who knew her records, she had a special

treat production number in which she appeared from doors cut in a giant record-cutting machine, singing one of her hit songs. When the song was through, she would explain the mechanics of the machine and then sing another hit. Lights that changed their colors would play upon her sequined white gown. There she would stand—tall and solid, singing masterfully, a queen of the blues.

To be at the top of blues popularity in those days was a difficult feat, because in black America the blues were all the rage, and many blues fans had other favorites beside Bessie. Country blues men like Charlie Patton and Blind Lemon Jefferson were recording. Ma Rainey was now recording, as well as Alberta Hunter and Ethel Waters. Strangely enough, besides Bessie, five of the most popular women had the last name of Smith, although none were related. Mamie, Trixie, Ada, Laura, and Clara Smith were all much sought after blues singers of the twenties. Bessie knew all of their reputations and their recorded work. Of this group, Bessie became close friends only with Clara who was, next to Bessie and Ma, perhaps the finest of all the singers. Bessie's competitive, scuffling spirit drove her on. She was determined to make her audiences forget that anyone else sang blues but her. She was destined to attain that height of Empress of the Blues over the next few years. The key to it lay in making records.

As winter came on, the tremendously successful Harlem Follies folded its tent, and Bessie returned to

New York to record. In those sessions she began to encounter the kind of supporting instrumentalists for whom she'd been looking for a long while. They were jazz players, not just show bandsmen. Jazz was a form as young almost as the blues, and an atmosphere of electricity surrounded sessions between Bessie and these young explorers. They listened to what was being sung or played and worked their musical lines in and out of hers with great skill. The great Charlie "Long Boy" Green became her favorite trombonist. Long Green could slur up and down on his instrument like a symphony orchestra player or quack and growl like a comical human voice when Bessie wanted some hokum in an arrangement. The talented Fred Longshaw became Bessie's tour-show pianist and band leader and helped her write several of her songs. Other pianists—Fletcher Henderson and the great James P. Johnson—soon won her admiration. And young Joe Smith, whose trumpet sound could sing like a blues singer's, could do no wrong as far as Bessie was concerned. Surrounded by these and many other great musicians, Bessie was recording hit after hit and beginning to leave the pretenders to her crown in the dust.

In 1925, Fred Longshaw and Frank Walker, who had become her personal business manager, advised and almost insisted that Bessie give up Joe Smith for the moment and cut a series of records with the great Louis Armstrong. Now Bessie was all set to show her top form on records with flawless accompaniment.

But she was stubborn when it came to her music, and she was not pleased at the substitution of trumpet men. Louis was only twenty-five years old, but he was an absolute ruler in the jazz trumpet world. His musical ideas were as strong as Bessie's, and she feared that he might try to blow her out of the studio with his big sound and ruin the performance. But she hadn't counted on Satchmo's excellent taste. As a musician accompanying a singer he knew just what to do. She finally accepted him, and he played lines that melted right in and lifted Bessie's lines as if his improvisations were a male dancer raising a prima ballerina on high. With Longshaw on the little pedal organ known as the harmonium and with Louis on cornet, Bessie recorded a version of W. C. Handy's "St. Louis Blues" that became a high-point recording of jazz history.

These were exhilarating times for Bessie. Jackie was gathering a new show to go out on tour. They had money to burn. They decided to buy something in which to carry the show around the country. Jack and Bessie went down to Atlanta and Jack took five thousand dollars cash out to the railroad yards there and bought a seventy-two-foot railroad car. On the side of it was painted JACK GEE PRESENTS BESSIE SMITH—THE EMPRESS OF THE BLUES. It was just like that—it was that impulsive, it was that matter-of-fact. Bessie's money flowed out as fast as her popularity rushed in.

Bessie was drinking more gin than she should have and when she drank she would either get mean or depressed with the blues mood. But she was basically happy in those days. She began writing her own blues and the results were excellent. Some of the best songs she sang were her own compositions. Usually she would only write the words and melody and have the pianist—Longshaw or Clarence Williams or Fletcher Henderson—make up harmony. And there were occasions when she'd sit down at the piano and pick out words, melody, and chords herself. "Reckless Blues," "Dixie Flyer Blues," "Soft Pedal Blues," "Baby Doll," and "Lonesome Desert Blues" came into being. Many were about how she felt or had once felt, but in most of them she tried to write about what would be most real to the hearts of her audiences— poor, hard-working southerners or equally hardpressed, "down-home" folks who had moved into the harsh and confusing maze of big northern cities.

Up on that stage night after night Bessie began to realize what power she had over the moods of her audiences—her people. When she roared into a rousing, happy song like "Hot Time" or "Cake Walking Babies," unleashing at the end a whole line of strutting, yelling dancers, she would begin to feel like the leader of some royal entourage bringing gold to the downtrodden. And when the lights came down she would moan out, in perfect articulation, words that touched their hearts and brought a hush over the house—"Trouble, trouble, I've seen it all my days," or "Any sound-minded woman's liable to go insane / When the last friend she's got has gone and caught a train." She would look out into the audience and realize how much a great performer was like a spiritual cook feeding the hungry. Bessie always loved to give presents, and now with a nation of poor blacks idolizing her presence and art, she was in a position to give the gift most appreciated—the gift of uplift through the beauty of song.

Bessie Was Mean and Bessie Was Kind

The power that she felt as empress of the blues inspired Bessie, but it also frightened her. People loved her, but sometimes she became afraid that they would stop loving her, that they would find a singer whom they would like better. Sometimes she became suspicious that people close to her only stuck with her for her prestige and money. Sometimes she just wanted to get away to a quiet place and leave the world behind. She bought a farm in New Jersey and spent some time there. But Bessie was not satisfied.

Bessie was drinking harder these days. When she felt frightened she drank gin, and she was, it seems, frightened a lot of the time in those years of 1926 and 1927. And when Bessie was drinking she could be evil. She could punch people, throw things, and fire people who worked for her, sending a hail of cursing after them as they fled.

She would often become jealous of Jackie at those

times. One night in the dressing room before a show, Bessie kissed Jackie and went out to the stage to perform. When the show was over she returned to the dressing room, and when she saw the side of Jackie's face covered with lipstick, she stopped a moment and began to frown. Not saying a word, she balled up her fist and almost knocked Jack onto the floor with a stiff left to the jaw. "Who you been sneakin' around with, Jackie? Whose lipstick is that?" she shouted.

"Hold on, baby. Don't you remember kissing me before the show?" said the startled Jack Gee. Bessie began to cry and apologized profusely, covering his face with more kisses. "Hand me a towel, darling," said Jack after the kisses were through. "I don't want you to hit me with your right hand, too."

She was becoming rough to live with and work with. Clarey could do nothing with her, and the two of them began to grow apart. The third man she trusted in the world besides Jack and Clarey was her manager, Frank Walker. Frank these days was spending a lot of time watching over Bessie. At one point he took twenty thousand dollars out of her earnings and put it into the bank for her. He also convinced her to buy a house for herself in Philadelphia. He feared that bad times might come upon her the way she was living, and he wanted her provided for. Often he would visit the Gees in Philadelphia, and Bessie would cook dinner, and then Frank would start his old plea, "Don't spend your money so fast,

Bessie. Try not to drink so much, Bessie. Be good to yourself."

But Bessie couldn't stop. She did listen to one piece of advice, however. Frank insisted that she never come to the recording sessions with gin in her. On the few occasions when she appeared at the studio drunk, Frank would cancel the session. Her records were her testament of greatness to the world, and she knew that they must be perfect. One of her best and favorite pianists was Fletcher Henderson, a classically trained and college-educated musician. In 1926 he wrote "The Gin House Blues" for Bessie, and she immediately went to work on it. At the recording session for "The Gin House Blues," Bessie sang with all the deep feeling and notes of misery of someone telling his life story.

> I've got those worst kind of gin house blues.
> I've got those worst kind of gin house blues.
> I make one trip there to see if I can ease my mind.
> And if I do I'm goin' to make it my last time.*

But a year later Bessie fought with Fletcher and broke with him for good.

Bessie began to argue with and lose a lot of friends and associates. On stage she often was so drunk that she could hardly stand up to sing her blues. When she'd stagger off, she'd grab Jack and want to take off

* Copyright 1926 by Tune-House, Inc. Copyright renewed 1953 and assigned to Alamo Music, Inc., New York, N.Y.

for a bar. In the bars she would often end up throwing punches at somebody. But a moment later, she'd say "Come on, let's have a drink." Bessie was like that— inside that one great frame two people fighting for control of one body and one mind. She was a confused, confusing, and complicated person. When the gin was out of her, she was the tenderest and kindest of people.

Frank Walker lived in Long Beach, Long Island, with his wife and little son, Johnny. Johnny became quite ill in the summer of 1926, and the Walkers feared for his life. One day, when Bessie was supposed to have been out on tour, she showed up at the door of the Walker home with her bags. Mrs. Walker answered the door. And Bessie spoke up in a way that wouldn't take no for an answer, "I'm Bessie Smith. You've got enough to do just taking care of your boy, so I thought I'd better come take care of everything else." Whereupon she moved in and shopped, cooked, and cleaned for the family until Johnny was well again.

At another time Bessie decided it was time to realize one of her lifelong dreams. She wanted her family moved out of Chattanooga. She and Jack went over to Kater Street, which was a short street running behind the Standard Theatre, and bought the houses at 1143 and 1141. "Sugar," she said to Jack, "I want you to go down to Tennessee and get my family." Jack made two trips and finally had transported Vi and Vi's daughter Laura, and Tinnie, Lulu, and all their children and possessions up North. Bessie could rest easier at last.

Bessie's great heart—even now as her personal behavior was getting worse—caused her to turn toward songs that expressed her concern for "her people." And her great trust in music led her to choose many songs that reflected her own life. If no song existed to say what she wanted said, she wrote one.

She wrote one of her finest blues compositions after traveling near the Mississippi River at the time of great floods. She was horrified to see thousands, who doubtless had once sat and cheered her, homeless and hungry. She felt helpless herself. Something about all this didn't seem fair, something didn't seem right. She became obsessed with the need to contribute something. The contribution was "Back Water Blues" and she wrote it on the train as she and Jack rode northward from Alabama to Chattanooga:

When it rained five days and the sky turned dark as night.
When it rained five days and the sky turned dark as night.
Then Trouble takin' place in the lowlands that night.

When it thundered and lightnen'd and the wind began to blow.
When it thundered and lightnen'd and the wind began to blow.

There's thousands of people didn't have no place to
go.

Then I went and stood on some high old lonesome
hill
Then I went and stood on some high old lonesome
hill
And looked down on the house where I used to live.

Back Water blues done caused me to pack my things
and go.
Back Water blues done caused me to pack my things
and go.
Cause my house fell down, and I can't go there no
more.

And in "Homeless Blues" the flood theme reappeared:

My ma and pa was drownded, Mississippi, you're to
blame
My ma and pa was drownded, Mississippi, you're to
blame
Mississippi, I can't stand to hear your name.

Her "Poor Man's Blues," though it looked back ten
years to World War I in its lyrics, was a plea to rich
men—the white world to her—for some compas-
sion for the poor:

Mr. rich man, rich man, open up your heart and mind.
Mr. rich man, rich man, open up your heart and mind.
Give a poor man a chance, help stop these hard times.

While you're living in your mansion, you don't know what hard times mean
While you're living in your mansion, you don't know what hard times mean
Home workin' man's wife is starving—Your wife is livin' like a queen.

Please listen to my pleadin' cause I can't stand these hard times long.
Please listen to my pleadin' cause I can't stand these hard times long.
They'll make an honest man do things that you know is wrong.

Poor man fought all the battles; poor man would fight again today
Poor man fought all the battles; poor man would fight again today
He would do anything you ask him in the name of the U.S.A.

And in "Preachin' the Blues," despite its slight air of humor, Bessie put forth a kind of religious statement.

In it she proposed an alternative to church-going and to asking for spiritual uplift from preachers and deacons.

> Preach them blues; sing them blues; they certainly
>   sound good to me.
> I been in love for the last six months and ain't done
>   worryin' yet . . .
> Moan them blues; holler them blues:
> Let me convert your soul.

The legend of "Big-hearted Bessie," as Jack Gee called her, ran through the land from New York to Los Angeles. You could see Bessie on big city streets time and again run into a group of poor street urchins and bending down, say, "Come here, Sugar. Let Bessie see if she's got some money for you all." In streets across the nation where Bessie had walked, one could hear some down-at-the-heels guy say to his companions, "I'll bet when Miss Bessie comes to town, I'll get me some money."

And Bessie gave it. She bought a house for the use of friends she felt sorry for. She would give a hundred dollars to people who'd begged for five. She got two fellows out of jail in Detroit, because their sister had come to her crying. She bought drinks around, fed, clothed, helped out, and generally fought a losing battle against the misery of her people. That feeling that somebody—God, the white man, Mr. Blues—

90

was making things unfair for her people and herself drove her toward setting things right with what she had—genius and money.

The end of the twenties was approaching, and Bessie was about to have a run of hard times. As a matter of fact the entire world was about to have a spell of bad luck. Bessie and the U.S.A. were just finishing the swinging, good-time era known as the "roaring twenties." And they were about to go down together.

IV
How Bessie Lost Her Empire and How She Died

Mr. Blues and the Depression

Bessie and Jack Gee took one more show out, but they were alone no longer. Mr. Blues went along this time. He bothered them only occasionally—after they had some nasty fight, or when Bessie downed a whole pint of gin and refused to perform. Midnight Steppers, as their show was christened, was a mighty success with the great James P. Johnson acting as pianist and artistic director. Had Bessie and Jackie saved the earnings from it, they might have lived comfortably for a long time, despite the Crash and the ensuing Depression. But it was not to be. Thousands of dollars were made and thousands were spent as the Steppers toured from coast to coast. On Bessie's dressing room table sat a box filled to the brim with diamonds and precious stones. In her closet were rich furs.

Bessie had grown tired of Frank Walker's endless counsel and nagging and had told him that Jackie would henceforth be her business manager. Jack was intelligent and had Bessie's best interest at heart, but he was not a professional business agent nor was he far enough removed from Bessie's personal life to give objective personal advice. Bessie still thought of Frank as a good friend, but she was now free to spend her money as she chose. At her very first recording session in 1923 a frightened Bessie Smith had sung, "If my friend ain't got no money / And I say 'Take all mine, honey' / Ain't nobody's business if I do: If I give him my last nickel / And it leaves me in a pickle / Ain't nobody's business if I do." Frank thought back to those words now, as Bessie dismissed him with an imperial shrug. He was out, he was sorry, and that was that.

Bessie was in need of business advice in those days, for as usual, there were two notions tugging with almost equal strength at her—this time about the question of what kind of music to record. By the end of the twenties the great classic blues craze was beginning to die out in the black communities. Bessie had sung the blues since she was a child, and they were her music. She and Ma Rainey had raised those blues from infancy, nurtured them, and Bessie had polished them and given them a king's outfit. Part of Bessie wanted to record nothing but blues. But the other part of her wanted to remain popular. To be popular from 1926 on meant that you had to sing songs that sounded more like what the radio was broadcasting. It was what her people were hearing when they turned on their hard-earned new radios. Being popular also meant making movies. Bessie starred in a short and shoddy film called *St. Louis Blues,* but the film was never released.

Bessie began recording show tunes and non-blues hits of the time. "After You've Gone," Irving Berlin's classic "Alexander's Ragtime Band," and lesser, corny songs like "Muddy Waters" and "Trombone Cholly." Bessie, great artist that she was, transformed each of these into magnificent music, but the public did not buy them in the mad-rush fashion that they had bought her old blues renditions. They loved her most for her blues and identified her with the blues, but they wanted something new. National radio networks began beaming out music designed to help the country forget the government's helplessness in avoiding the Great Depression, which was just beginning, and Bessie's people began liking the idea. They began liking lighthearted, tinselly tunes, sung by light-voiced, tinselly radio singers. The blues empire was crashing down, and the people were leaving Bessie and her blue land of frustration songs.

Bessie, who had been commanding $2,000 to $3,000 a week in 1928, was beginning to work for less and less money. Of course, her behavior was no help to her financial situation. Many theater owners, tired of her drunkenness and unreliability, refused to book her, and she started accepting roles in cheap musical shows and singing in joints unbefitting her great artistry. After the Crash of 1929, even Bessie's

97

hardiest admirers found themselves without the seventy-five cents to buy records or the fifty cents to get a ticket for her tour performances. The T.O.B.A. fell apart.

Jack and Bessie did not survive all of this chaos. They just couldn't. All of the turmoil and doubts, the losses and accusations that you'd expect at a time when financial props were being knocked out from under not only Bessie but the whole country, worked with tragic consequences upon the almost unreal married life that these two high-living show people had experienced. After several years of arguing and fighting the two of them—Bessie, full to her eyelids with gin, and Jack, full of overblown self-confidence —separated officially in 1930, strangely enough without a fight but with a tired-out kind of resignation.

Jack and Bessie were two super-stubborn beings, and although they were in constant touch for the rest of Bessie's life, they never took up their marriage again. Jack often thought of many things that had passed during their intense life together. Perhaps as much as anything else, he recalled the times they had run into Ma Rainey in the late twenties. He remembered the big affectionate bear hugs those two giants of the blues had given one another. But echoing in his mind many a night were Ma's usual parting words to Jack, "That's my daughter there. You take good care of her." At those times Jack often wept and blamed himself bitterly for having lost her and for not knowing any more about her than that she was in the world somewhere.

Bessie was on the road somewhere. She was singing for carnivals and in cabarets and in half-empty theaters. She was in Chicago. She was in New Orleans. She was in Selma. In June 1931 she was in New York for one of her last recording sessions. Things had changed. But not Frank, as he lent her as much money as he had and glowed again at the great genius that thrust itself undaunted through her gin-roughened old voice. What had changed was that nobody expected any huge hit from this session. What had also changed was that a "dyin'-by-the-hour" look had come into Long Green's weathered face. And the exuberant little trumpet man Joe Smith wasn't there. His health had failed him, and he was out on Long Island in a hospital where he would die three years later.

Bessie sang two of her own compositions at that session, two songs that sent a chill up Frank's back as he thought of their thinly veiled implications. "Ship-wreck Blues" and "Long Old Road"—bitterness was in them and death. "I don't want to depress all those people with singing these blues," she had often said, but that day she sang them, almost roaring out the words.

It's cloudy outdoors as it can be.
That's the time I need my good man with me.
It's rainin' and it's stormin' on the sea.

It's rainin' and it's stormin' on the sea.
I feel like somebody had shipwrecked for me.

And then echoed in "Long Old Road":

You can't trust nobody; you might as well be alone.
You can't trust nobody; you might as well be alone.
And my long, lost friend and I might as well have
stayed at home.

Bessie went back to her lonesome road. A few months later she received the news that Long Green had been found in a Harlem doorway one morning, frozen to death. Not long after that, Bessie was called to the graveside of her niece Laura, Viola's daughter, who was almost Bessie's own age. Bessie stood there as the casket was being lowered into the grave. "I'm next," she said softly and walked away.

Bessie walked away from Laura's grave into her own nightmare. By this point she had given up hope for a resurgence of her career. She was no longer performing for the uplift of her people—she *was* her people. She was out of work a lot of the time. She drifted. She lived from day to day. She was lost within a situation she could not control. And in a sense, she was worse off than the multitude of jobless, poor people who now in the 1930's stood in line to receive free soup and bread, because she had once been up on the mountaintop. It sounds crazy, but maybe the words she wrote long ago in "Back Water Blues" drifted through her mind:

> Then I went and stood on some high old lonesome hill.
> Then I went and stood on some high old lonesome hill.
> And looked down on the house where I used to live.

The blues were dead. Frank Walker himself had said it, and Bessie had seen evidence of their death everywhere she went. People on street corners were not whistling the old moaning, twelve-bar blues: they were whistling innocent little ditties about sunshine and smiling and looking for silver linings. The sales from the two records she made in 1931 hardly paid for the players and the pressing. The radio, the movies, the musicals—everybody was breaking his neck trying to appear happy—as the world drifted through the Great Depression. Bessie tried it herself for about five minutes, but she felt foolish. She had lost too much—love, wealth, and a kingdom of adulation. She decided not to care any more. She went under. She drank gin by the pint whenever she felt that she was about to care, to worry, to feel remorse, to cry. Whenever she needed some money, she would wander around until her once-great reputation would land her a job—for old times' sake. She sang in dives and played "mammy" parts in stage productions. Every now and then she would be hired for a

101

fairly large sum of money to sing a few pornographic songs.

Once in New York she was even invited to sing the old songs at a jam session held at the Onyx Club. She walked in wrapped in a beat-up old fur coat, but she still carried herself like the empress. Not even doffing her coat, she roared out a few songs and left as suddenly as she'd come. Old timers who heard her there speak of that performance in superlatives to this day.

Gin and hard times had put a growl into Bessie's voice, but she couldn't have sung badly even if all her vocal chords could do was howl and bark. The Depression and her compulsive self-destruction could never prevail over her musical genius, her understanding of her words, her mastery over a line of notes.

From time to time Bessie pulled herself together and tried to gather some hope. But it was hard. It was hard to be sober, to sit alone in her room in some big, concrete northern city and plan out a new career, to let the old blues, indeed, slip away into the graveyard, to avoid thinking of Jackie and the Midnight Steppers and Bud and Laura and Mama Laura and the one dollar with its double eagles, won at the Star Theatre.

Well, the blues might be dead; but Bessie knew well that Mr. Blues was on stage—the man of the hour.

Route 61 and the Death of Bessie Smith

Once I lived the life of a millionaire.
Spending my money, I didn't care.
I carried my friends out for a good time,
Buying boot-leg liquor, champagne, and wine.
Then I began to fall so low
I didn't have a friend and no place to go.
And if I ever get my hands on a dollar again,
I'm going to hold on to it till those eagles grin.

Nobody knows you,
When you're down and out.
In my pockets not one penny,
And my friends I haven't any.
But if I ever get on my feet again,
Then I'll meet my long, lost friends.

It's mighty strange, without a doubt—
Nobody knows you when you're down and out.

It was September 1937. Jack Gee was staying at his mother's apartment on 135th Street in New York. It was nighttime and the tall former policeman, who had stepped out for the evening, wearily climbed the gloomy stairs to the apartment, unlocked the door, and walked a few steps down the long unlit hall that led to his bedroom. Suddenly he found himself on the floor. "Doggone it! Who left these bags in this hall? Ma! Ma! Who . . . ."

"Bessie's in your room, Jack. You better go on in," said Mrs. Gee.

Jackie went into his little bedroom and turned on the light. "Bessie!" he shouted with a start in spite of having been warned of her presence. "What are you doin' in my bed, gal?" They both laughed.

"I thought I'd surprise you, sugar," said Bessie in girlish glee. "Wait, hon, before you take your shoes off—would you mind running down to the store and buying me a Coca-Cola?"

Jack was delighted. Few people besides him would ever believe that Bessie drank almost as much Coke as she drank gin. He was glad she was having the Coke by itself. When he had returned and joined her in bed and she had finished her soft drink, Bessie lay back and began to talk. She seemed to have recovered the brightness in her eye that Jack had loved her for when they were both young. Bessie rambled, talking in uncommonly optimistic terms about the trend of the last few years in her life. She spoke of the kindness that a young New York jazz critic by the name of

John Hammond had shown her, when late in 1933 he had set up a recording session for her. She spoke of how a small crowd of jazz lovers—and most of them white folks—had started getting enthusiastic about her work. "You know I was a hit at Connie's Inn," she added. She said she had plans, that Hammond was setting up another recording date for her next month. She spoke of a tour that she was supposed to make through a string of large movie houses and about a film in which she would star. Her eyes shone brightly there in the dark room. The night hours ticked away.

"Sugar, I need your advice. The Silas Green Show is doing a run through the South, and they want me to appear. It'll be two hundred and fifty dollars for only five minutes a night. It sounds good, Jack. Don't you think? Baby, it's all starting to click again, Bessie's on the comeback trail. And I'm licking that old, nasty habit of mine . . . you know, gin?"

They shared a laugh. "It sounds wonderful, Baby. I suppose you ought to go on down there and start getting that gorgeous voice of yours back up where it belongs," said Jack.

Her friend Richard was driving. The show that night in Darling, Mississippi, had been a smash hit. Bessie sat back and rode easy as the old Packard rolled along under heavy trees. The night was warm, and Bessie's elbow rested lightly on the open window frame. Her thoughts had always been crowded

with little phrases of music—a groan, a snatch of
rhyme from a song. Tonight they were coming thick
and fast.

> I went to the gypsy to get my fortune told.
> She said you in hard luck, Bessie, Dog-gone your
>   hard-luck soul!!!

It was 1:10 A.M. September 25, 1937.

Bessie was in her thirty-ninth year. She had squan-
dered over a million dollars in her time. She had
made

> No father to guide me, no mother to care . . .
> Must bear my troubles all alone . . .

over seven million dollars for Columbia, ten million
records sold. In 1923

> Gypsy don't hurt him, but fix him for me one more
>   time.
> Just make him love me, Gypsy, But please take him
>   off my mind.

her sales saved Columbia from going

bankrupt.

It had been a beautiful fall

Some people call me a hobo, some call me a bum
Nobody knows my name, nobody knows what I've
    done.

day . . . on their way to Memphis.

I'm as good as any woman in your town . . . .
I want to be somebody's baby doll,
So I can get my lovin' all the time.

They were on a dark Route 61, ten miles from
Clarksdale, Mississippi.

But if I ever get on my feet again,
Then I'll find my long-lost friends.

Richard sat quietly at the wheel. They approached
a little rise

107

Got the blues so bad, I can see Death Valley, and I
    can't do nothin' but cry.
Please tell me, Mr. Blues, have you brought me here
    to die?

in the road. Suddenly parked there on the highway
was a truck marked NATIONAL BISCUIT CO.

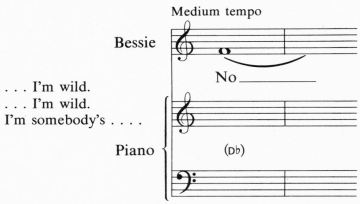

Richard hit the brakes; the car tires screamed and
there was nothing more to do. Steel smacked into
steel, glass smashed, baggage flew, lights went out.
Richard was in a dream. Bessie was moaning something, God knows what. A few cars passed. After
some time a car pulled up. A man jumped out. He
was white. He was on his way fishing. He said he
was a doctor. They rushed to Bessie, lying in the
road, to move her. Bessie was heavy. One of her
arms was all but torn off at the elbow. She was
bleeding profusely. The young doctor bandaged
Bessie as well as he could. Suddenly the doctor's

car was hit by another car approaching from the rear. And suddenly there was not just Bessie hurt and mangled on the road. There were the passengers of the other car. Route 61 was wet with blood. It was a long time before a driver came along that tranquil highway and, witnessing the tragic scene, drove on into town for help.

Finally several ambulances arrived. One ambulance rushed off toward Clarksdale, ten miles away, with Bessie and Richard inside. When they arrived at the large hospital in Clarksdale, the officials at the emergency ward informed Richard that they would not treat Negroes but that they could be helped at the G. T. Thomas Hospital and Funeral Home in the same town. Time passed. Bessie was bleeding to death.

They arrived at the G. T. Thomas Hospital. Bessie was dying by the minute, but was semiconscious. The attendant doctor began working on her. It was 12:15 P.M. when someone heard her say, "I'm going, but I'm going in the name of the Lord." Others said they were not sure. She gasped. She shuddered. She slipped away.

Clarence Smith sent to Clarksdale for the remains of his sister. Her body was carried north alone on a train. Clarey, Frank, and Jackie stood above the grave as Bessie Smith was lowered and buried in Philadelphia at Mt. Lawn Cemetery on October 4, 1937.

THE CHICAGO DEFENDER

Saturday, October 9, 1937

Bessie Smith Is Buried in Philadelphia

LONG LINE OF MOURNERS
PAY LAST RESPECTS TO BLUES SINGER

By JAMES M. REID

PHILADELPHIA, Oct. 8—Bessie Smith, "Queen" of the blues and the grandest trouper of them all, answered her final curtain call. She was buried here Monday in Mt. Lawn Cemetery.

Brought to an untimely death through an automobile accident in Clarksdale, Miss., where she was appearing in a stage show last week, the "Queen" took her last bow before the footlights and received the last respects of an admiring public and the homage of her theatrical colleagues in a simple but very impressive funeral service at the O. V. Catto Elks home, Sixteenth and Fitzwater streets.

Mourned by All

Bessie Smith was dressed in a gorgeous flesh lace gown with pink slippers. She rested in an expensive open silver metallic casket trimmed in gold and draped in a two-toned velvet lining.

Being the first of the Race to have professional pallbearers in Philadelphia, the body was borne on the shoulders of the men out of the hall and a block down Sixteenth Street between tightly packed rows of people, preceded by the choir softly intoning "Rest in Peace," to the waiting hearse.

Mate Grief Stricken

The "Queen" leaves to mourn her demise, husband-manager and companion, Jack Gee, three sisters and one brother, all living in Philadelphia: they are Viola, Tinnie, Lulu and Clarence Smith.

The body of Bessie Smith lay in state all day Sunday at the funeral home of William Upshur. Thousands of people passed the bier to view the remains of a great star. . . .

110

BLUES COMPOSITIONS AND LYRICS
BY BESSIE SMITH

(Available through Empress Music Inc. New York, New York)

Baby Doll
Back Water Blues
Blue Blues
Cake Walking Babies from Home
Death Valley Moan
Dirty No-gooder's Blues
Dixie Flyer Blues
Foolish Man Blues
Golden Rule Blues
Good Feelin' Blues
He's Gone Blues
High Water Blues
In the House Blues
Lonesome Desert Blues
Long Old Road
Lost Your Head Blues
My Man Blues
Pick Pocket Blues
Please Help Me Get Him Off My Mind
Poor Man's Blues
Preachin' the Blues
Reckless Blues
Rocking Chair Blues
Shipwreck Blues
Spider Man Blues (Harold Gray and Bessie Smith)
Soft Pedal Blues
Sorrowful Blues
Standin' in the Rain Blues
Sweet Potato Blues
Telephone Blues
Thinking Blues
Wasted Life Blues
Young Woman's Blues

SELECTED DISCOGRAPHY

COLUMBIA RECORDS LP: "THE BESSIE SMITH STORY,"
VOLS. I—IV

CL 855—Bessie Smith with Louis Armstrong

Down Hearted Blues	Feb. 15, 1923
Jailhouse Blues	Sept. 21, 1923
Ticket Agent Ease Your Window Down	April 7, 1923
St. Louis Blues	Jan. 24, 1925
Reckless Blues	Jan. 24, 1925
You've Been a Good Ole Wagon	Jan. 24, 1925
Sobbin' Hearted Blues	Jan. 24, 1925
Cold in Hand Blues	Jan. 24, 1925
Careless Love Blues	May 26, 1925
Nashville Woman's Blues	May 26, 1925
I Ain't Gonna Play No Second Fiddle	May 27, 1925
J. C. Holmes Blues	May 27, 1925

CL 856—Bessie Smith, Blues to Barrelhouse

Weeping Willow Blues	Sept. 26, 1924
Jazzbo Brown from Memphis Town	March 18, 1926
The Gin House Blues	March 18, 1926
Poor Man's Blues	Aug. 24, 1928
Me and My Gin	Aug. 25, 1929
Nobody Knows You When You're Down and Out	May 25, 1929

112

New Orleans Hop Scop Blues	March 27, 1930
Black Mountain Blues	July 22, 1930
Gimme a Pigfoot	Nov. 24, 1933
Take Me for a Buggy Ride	Nov. 24, 1933
Do Your Duty	Nov. 24, 1933
I'm Down in the Dumps	Nov. 24, 1933

CL 857—With Joe Smith and Fletcher Henderson's Hot Six

Cake Walking Babies	May 5, 1925
The Yellow Dog Blues	May 5, 1925
At the Christmas Ball	Nov. 18, 1925
Baby Doll	May 4, 1926
Money Blues	May 4, 1926
Lost Your Head Blues	May 4, 1926
One and Two Blues	Oct. 10, 1926
Young Woman's Blues	Oct. 10, 1926
Alexander's Ragtime Band	March 2, 1927
Muddy Water	March 2, 1927
After You've Gone	March 2, 1927
There'll Be a Hot Time in Old Town Tonight	March 2, 1927

CL 858—With James P. Johnson and Charlie Green

Back Water Blues	Feb. 17, 1927
Preachin' the Blues	Feb. 17, 1927
He's Got Me Goin'	Aug. 20, 1929
Blue Spirit Blues	Oct. 11, 1929
Moan, Mourners	June 9, 1930
On Revival Day	June 9, 1930

113

Trombone Cholly	March 3, 1927
Send Me to the 'lectric Chair	March 3, 1927
Empty Bed Blues	March 20, 1928
Long Old Road	June 11, 1931
Shipwreck Blues	June 11, 1931

Also

GERTRUDE "MA" RAINEY: MOTHER OF THE BLUES
Riverside Records, Inc.; RM 8807

BIBLIOGRAPHY

AVAKIAN, GEORGE. "The Bessie Smith Story," Liner notes. Columbia Records Corp., New York.

The Chicago Defender, 1922–1938.

HADLOCK, RICHARD. "Bessie Smith," *Jazz Masters of the Twenties.* New York: The Macmillan Company, 1965.

HOEFER, GEORGE. "Bessie Smith," *The Jazz Makers.* New York: Rinehart and Co., 1957.

The Jazz Record, September 1947.

JONES, LEROI. *Blues People.* New York: William Morrow and Co., 1963.

KEEPNEWS, ORRIN, AND GRAUER, WILLIAM. *A Pictorial History of Jazz.* New York: Crown Publishers, 1966.

KEIL, CHARLES. *Urban Blues.* Chicago: University of Chicago Press, 1966.

OLIVER, PAUL. *Bessie Smith.* New York: A. S. Barnes and Co., 1961.

SCHULLER, GUNTHER. "Bessie Smith." *Early Jazz,* vol. I. New York: Oxford University Press, 1968.

WATERS, ETHEL: *His Eye Is on the Sparrow.* Garden City, N.Y.: Doubleday & Co., 1951.

INDEX

INDEX

F. C. Woolcott's Rabbit Foot Minstrel Show, 16

G. T. Thomas Hospital and Funeral Home, 109
Gee, Jackie, 61-66, 68, 70-72, 73-74, 75-76, 84, 85, 86, 90, 102, 104-105, 109, 110
  involvement in career of Bessie Smith, 73-74, 75-76, 80, 95-96
  marries Bessie Smith, 70
  separation from Bessie Smith, 98-99
"Gin House Blues, The," 85
Green, Charlie "Long Boy," 79, 99, 100
"Gulf-Coast Blues," 69, 71

Hamilton, Bob, 76
Hammond, John, 105
Handy, W. C., 80
Harlem Follies Troupe, 75-78
Henderson, Fletcher, 79, 81, 85
"Homesick Blues," 88
Horan's (Philadelphia), 61-63
"How Come You Do Me Like You Do," 71

Hunter, Alberta, 56, 68, 78

Ivory Theatre (Chattanooga), 11, 16
"I Wish I Could Shimmy Like My Sister Kate," 56, 65

Jaxon, Half-Pint, 56
jazz, 54, 79
Jefferson, Blind Lemon, 78
Johnson, James P., 79, 95

Kern, Jerome, 54

Lafayette Theatre (Harlem), 75
Liberty Belles, the, 52, 53
"Lonesome Desert Blues," 81
"Long Old Road," 99, 100
Longshaw, Fred, 79, 80, 81
Lou (Pot of Peas), 76, 77

Martin, Sara, 56
Midnight Steppers, 95, 102
Morgan, Richard, 105, 107, 108, 109
motion pictures, 54, 97
Mt. Lawn Cemetery (Philadelphia), 109, 110
"Muddy Water," 97
Murphy, Min, 45-46

118

ABOUT THE AUTHOR

Carman Moore writes, "I am a classical music com-
poser but also a black man and a teacher. More im-
portantly I am a lover of the blues. I believe that the
blues is one of the enduring containers of artistic
creation—almost a century old in its most archaic
form." In 1967 Mr. Moore founded the first course on
the history of popular music at New York's New School
for Social Research to try to document some of the
non-European music that has so long been ignored
by scholars. SOMEBODY'S ANGEL CHILD is a natural
consequence of this interest.

Mr. Moore was born in Lorain, Ohio, and began
his musical studies at the Oberlin Conservatory while
he was still in high school in Elyria, Ohio. After grad-
uating from Ohio State University he came to New
York, where he received a master's degree in composition at Juilliard.

He has taught at the Dalton School, New York
University, and the New School for Social Research.
He is presently a lecturer at Manhattanville College
and the University of Connecticut. He was music
specialist for the Harlem Education Program, and a
consultant in Bedford-Stuyvesant for the Center for
Urban Education. He is now associate artistic director
with Gian Carlo Menotti of The Harlem Theatre and
Workshop. In addition Mr. Moore is music critic for
the *Village Voice* and has written reviews and arti-

cles for newspapers and magazines. With his wife and young son he now lives in New York City, and somehow finds time to write poetry and plays and enjoy tennis and touch football as well.